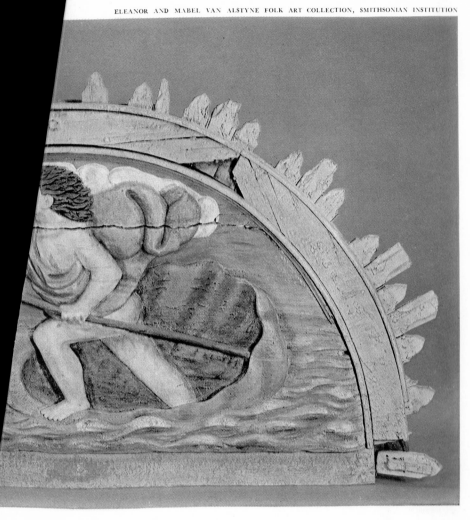

ars before the Civil War, schoolboys and their
re so well versed in the classics that they would
no difficulty identifying the figure in this primi-
...ting as Neptune, the Roman god of the sea. It
one of the wooden shields that covered the paddle
of a steamboat called, of course, Neptune. She has
...ce steamed away to that great landing in the sky;
as recorded in the article beginning on page 54—
f her graceful successors have followed in her wake.

In the ya
elders we
have had
tive pai
adorned
wheels
long si
sadly—
most

AMERICAN HERITAGE

The Magazine of History

Sponsored by

American Association for State & Local History · Society of American Historians

CONTENTS *December, 1966 · Volume XVIII, Number 1*

AMERICAN HERITAGE is published every two months by American Heritage Publishing Co., Inc., 551 Fifth Avenue, New York, N.Y. 10017. Correspondence about subscriptions should be addressed to: American Heritage Subscription Office, 383 West Center Street, Marion, Ohio 43301. Single Copies $3.95. Annual Subscriptions: $15.00 in U.S. & Canada; $16.00 elsewhere.

An annual Index of AMERICAN HERITAGE is published every February, priced at $1.00. A Cumulative Index of Volumes VI–XV is available at $5.00.

AMERICAN HERITAGE will consider but assumes no responsibility for unsolicited material. Title registered U.S. Patent Office. Second-class postage paid at New York, N.Y., and at additional mailing offices.

COVER: The powerful bay gelding trotting briskly along in Scott Leighton's painting is St. Julien, driven by Orrin Hickok, brother of the famous Wild Bill. In October of 1879, performing at Oakland Park, California, before a huge crowd which included former President (and amateur horseman) Ulysses S. Grant, just returned from a triumphant trip around the world, St. Julien set a new world's trotting record of 2:12¾ for the mile. It was the heyday of harness racing; from Boston to San Francisco, horses and their drivers received the same kind of adulation that a later generation would accord Red Grange and Babe Ruth. Fortunately, it was also the heyday of American printmaking, when the exciting duels between these spirited animals were recorded in lithographs of surpassing beauty. An article about the era, accompanied by a portfolio of trotting prints, begins on page 30. Leighton's painting is in the collection of the Hall of Fame of the Trotter in Goshen, New York. *Back Cover:* Moderns distressed by advertising's use of pretty girls to push all kinds of products may be relieved to learn that the practice isn't new. But nowadays some advanced young ladies actually smoke the cigars; that would have shocked *everyone* in 1900. This label, lithographed by C. L. Schwencke of New York, is owned by Culver Pictures.

Beginning
a series
of articles
on
notable
American
trials

VERDICTS

"The law," declared Sir Edward Coke, is the "perfection of reason"; although to Mr. Bumble, the beadle of *Oliver Twist,* it could be, in its baffling workings, "a ass—a idiot." Much the same argument continues to this day, with the points of view relatively unchanged. No one respects law more, or argues more heatedly about it, than the English-speaking peoples. No one manufactures more of it, in sheer weight, bulk, and complexity, than the Americans. The law has reflected and sometimes accelerated the transition of the United States from a rural republic to a city-dwellers' democracy. And how has most of this law been made? Not, despite fond popular belief, in our legislatures, but in our courtrooms.

In the past few years, headline after headline has told us of judicial verdicts that banned official prayer from public schools, desegregated the classrooms, ordered state reapportionments that many think will open a new (if not necessarily better) era in American politics, and in recent rulings on confessions and search procedures, drastically altered the balance of power between the policeman and the accused. Some of the court decisions have represented what football writers might call "end runs" around the immovable lines of the Senate; some of them have probably represented the majority will of the country, and some of them probably have not. But they are all law, despite violent debates in newspapers and on the air, congressional speeches, and threats to amend the Constitution.

The courtroom has always been an arena in which opposing classes, ideas, and ways of life have met in direct conflict. Sometimes, as in Theodore Roosevelt's titanic confrontation with J. P. Morgan over the Northern Securities trust, the legal battle has averted a bloodier clash. In other cases, the courtroom ritual has only served to intensify hatreds. Textbook summaries have, for instance, almost totally obscured for us the enormous impact that John Brown's trial had on the popular mind in the North. Similarly, we have lost sight of the tragic mixture of justice and revenge that motivated the men who tried to impeach Andrew Johnson. Forgotten even more completely, because the principle is so well established, are several trials of the early 1800's in which Alexander Hamilton and others placed the free press out of reach of political attack.

In the trials of labor leaders such as Big Bill Heywood, arch criminals such as Al Capone, tycoons such as Samuel Insull, government officials such as Alger Hiss, an entire era is condensed, recapitulated—and judged. Often the verdict is like a pivot on which swings a vast change of public mood. Even a murder trial can produce a notable legal precedent along with its standard ingredients of vivid emotion and purple oratory—when, for instance, the man on trial is a romantic scoundrel like Congressman Daniel Sickles, and the victim is the son of Francis Scott Key. That trial, the sensation of 1859, established the "unwritten" law whereby wronged husbands and wives could revenge themselves with impunity.

The courtroom is also an incomparable crucible for distilling the essence of human character. To follow Lincoln, Hamilton, or Burr word for word before a jury gives us insight into a great personality that often cannot be achieved in any other way. From the opposite end of the telescope, trials of the past can give us new perspectives on similar issues in the present. The judgment on Abraham Lincoln's murderers, for instance, offers a hundred comparisons to the Warren Commission report on President Kennedy's death. Finally, by looking with a calm, objective eye on the verdicts that agitated other generations, we may be able to consider more dispassionately the judicial turmoil of our own time.

These are only a few of the rewards that we are confident readers will find in the new series which begins on the next page. It will be written by Thomas J. Fleming, distinguished author of *Now We Are Enemies* and *One Small Candle,* and a frequent contributor to AMERICAN HERITAGE.

Our opening article, the story of John Adams' defense of the British soldiers who shot down his fellow Bostonians one tumultuous March evening in 1770, a night in some ways reminiscent of Watts, and Detroit, and Cleveland, is a striking example of how courtroom drama can combine historical significance, deadly parallels, and enduring human interest.—*The Editors*

OF HISTORY

VERDICTS OF HISTORY I

Even the worst offender, even th
lawyer. Our example is a passionat
Revolution, when John Adam
British soldiers who had fired into
There are echoes of our ow

By THOMAS

"The Jurors for the said Lord the King upon oath present that Thomas Preston, Esq.; William Wemms, laborer; James Hartegan, laborer; William McCauley, laborer; Hugh White, laborer; Matthew Killroy, laborer; William Warren, laborer; John Carroll, laborer and Hugh Montgomery, laborer, all now resident in Boston in the County of Suffolk, . . . not having the fear of God before their eyes, but being moved and seduced by the instigation of the devil and their own wicked hearts, did on the 5th day of this instant March, at Boston aforesaid within the county aforesaid with force and arms feloniously, willfully and of their malice aforethought assault one Crispus Attucks, then and there being in the peace of God and of the said Lord the King and that the said William Warren, with a certain handgun of the value of 20 shillings, which he the said William Warren then and there held in both his hands charged with gunpowder and two leaden bullets, then and there feloniously, willfully and of his malice aforethought, did shoot off and discharge at and against the said Crispus Attucks, and that the said William Warren, with the leaden bullets as aforesaid out of the said handgun then and there by force of the said gunpowder so shot off and discharged as aforesaid did then and there feloniously, willfully and of his malice aforethought, strike, penetrate and wound the said Crispus Attucks in and upon the right breast a little below the right pap of him the said Crispus and in and upon the left breast a little below the left pap . . . of which said mortal wounds the said Crispus Attucks then and there instantly died."

THE BOSTON MASSACRE

ost unpopular cause, deserves a good
oment in Boston on the eve of the
ndertook to defend the hated
Boston mob and created some "martyrs."
mes in the trial that followed

EMING

Thus did the citizens of Boston indict nine British soldiers for murder. (The designation of the soldiers as "laborers" in the indictment emphasized that they were being tried as ordinary citizens—and also that they often eked out their pay by working for hire in and around Boston.) Never before in the history of Massachusetts had a trial aroused such intense, complex political and personal passion. Although his name stands alone in the indictment, Crispus Attucks was not the only victim. Four other Bostonians were also dead in what Samuel Adams, through his mouthpiece Benjamin Edes, publisher of the Boston *Gazette,* promptly called "a horrid massacre." For Adams and his friends in the Liberty party, the trial could have only one possible outcome. Paul Revere summed it up in the verse beneath his famous engraving of the scene.

> *But know, Fate summons to that awful Goal*
> *Where Justice strips the Murd'rer of his Soul:*
> *Should venal C[our]ts the scandal of the land*
> *Snatch the relentless Villain from her Hand*
> *Keen Execrations on this Plate inscrib'd*
> *Shall reach a Judge who never can be brib'd.*

The gist of what happened, whether baldly or passionately stated, was simple enough. Parliament's passage of the Townshend duties (import taxes on lead, paper, glass, tea) had inspired a series of riots and assaults on Royal officials which the magistrates and watchmen of Boston seemed helpless to prevent. On October 1, 1768, the Crown had landed two regiments

Paul Revere's famous engraving, from which these details come, gives a vivid if not quite detached view of the affray.

THE PROSECUTION: *Of the four principal lawyers who acted in the Boston Massacre trial, the one whose political sympathies leaned most toward the British soldiers was Samuel Quincy (left, as painted by John Singleton Copley). As solicitor general of Massachusetts, however, he was obliged to head the prosecution. When the Revolution came, he fled to the West Indies as a Loyalist. On the other hand, his associate counsellor, Robert Treat Paine (above), became a signer of the Declaration of Independence.*

of Royal troops to keep the peace. Relations between the townspeople and the soldiers had started poor and deteriorated steadily. After eighteen months, tempers on both sides were sputtering ominously.

Ironically, Parliament was about to repeal the Townshend duties, except for the tiny tax on tea, but the news had not reached Boston when the explosion occurred. At about eight o'clock on the moonlit night of March 5, 1770, a sentry on duty before the hated Custom House gave an impudent apprentice boy a knock on the ear with his gun. An unruly crowd gathered. Someone rang the bells in a nearby church. This signal, ordinarily a summons to fight fire, drew more people into the street. The frightened sentry called out the main guard. Seven men led by a corporal responded, and were shortly joined by Captain Thomas Preston. A few minutes later, a volley of shots left five "martyrs" dead or dying in the snow and six other men painfully wounded.

For a few hours Boston teetered on the brink of a blood bath. The well-armed Sons of Liberty outnumbered the British regiments ten to one, and the local

militia was swiftly bolstered by hundreds of farmers who swarmed in from the countryside. Only a desperate speech by Lieutenant Governor Thomas Hutchinson, in which he promised to arrest the soldiers and charge them with murder, calmed the enraged city enough to restore an uneasy semblance of peace.

On the morning after the bloodshed, John Adams was in his office beside the Town House steps. Through the door came a tearful, wailing man, James Forest, known about Boston as a British toady and scornfully called "the Irish infant." The accused leader of the arrested British soldiers, Captain Preston, had begged him to find a lawyer posthaste. This had proved very difficult. Finally, young Josiah Quincy, Jr., from John Adams' home town of Braintree, had expressed a willingness on one condition—that John Adams join him in the defense. One other lawyer, Robert Auchmuty, a staunch conservative, had volunteered with the same proviso.

The challenge aroused all the latent conservatism in the thirty-four-year-old John Adams' pugnacious spirit. For a decade he had watched his distant cousin Samuel

THE DEFENSE: *The chief defending attorneys were both, ironically, American patriots—one of them destined for the Presidency after a uniquely distinguished career. John Adams (right, as painted by Benjamin Blyth in 1763) was a close friend of both prosecutors; his wife, Abigail, was a Quincy cousin. Josiah Quincy, Jr. (above), his assistant, was Samuel's younger brother. He too might have been one of the Founding Fathers; but his patriotic ardor was cut short by death from tuberculosis in 1775.*

construct a "political engine" in Boston, discovering under his tutelage "the wheels . . . cogs or pins, some of them dirty ones, which composed the machine and made it go." Though he wrote convincing defenses of the Liberty party position in the Boston *Gazette,* John often signed himself "Clarendon" (the British lord who had done his utmost to prevent Cromwell's excesses in the English civil war), and politely declined to harangue town meetings in the demagogic style of cousin Samuel and his friends Dr. Joseph Warren and James Otis. John took an even dimmer view of the violent tendencies of the Sons of Liberty—and obviously saw a direct connection between their terrorist tactics and the frightened state of the Boston bar.

Years later, John Adams recalled that he had "no hesitation" in accepting the case. He told Forest "that Council ought to be the very last thing that an accused person should want [*i.e.,* lack] in a free country. That the bar ought in my opinion to be independent and impartial at all times and in every circumstance."

This was a noble ideal, but John Adams knew that it was far from the reality of Boston in 1770. The city was ruthlessly divided into King's men and Liberty men. Doctors, lawyers, even clergymen, were chosen for their fiercely partisan political opinions. Adams himself had made his irrevocable choice in 1768, when he refused Thomas Hutchinson's offer to make him advocate general of the Court of Admiralty. Since that time the vast proportion of his law practice had come from Liberty clients.

Nevertheless Adams solemnly accepted a guinea from James Forest as a retainer to seal the agreement. He warned the overwrought Irishman that this would be "as important a cause as had ever been tried in any court or country of the world." Neither he nor Captain Preston could, of course, expect anything more than "fact, evidence and law would justify."

"Captain Preston," Forest answered, "requested and desired no more . . . as God Almighty is my judge I believe him an innocent man."

It was only a few days before the surprising news of Adams' decision had made a complete circuit of Boston and its environs. Rocks were flung through the windows of the Adams home. Boys jeered him on the

THE JUDGES: *Of the four justices presiding at the Massacre trials, the three most prominent were inclined toward the Loyalist side. Benjamin Lynde (left) was a moderate; but Peter Oliver (center) was a firm King's man who after 1776 resided in England; while Edmund Trowbridge (right), a famous jurist, remained neutral in the Revolution despite his views.*
THE JURY: *John Adams managed to pack the jury with citizens sure to be unprejudiced against his clients. Loyalist Gilbert DeBlois (opposite page, in one of Copley's finer oil portraits) turned out to be a key man in Captain Preston's trial, in effect persuading the other jurors to vote for acquittal.*

streets. Josiah Quincy got a letter from his father in Braintree: "My Dear Son, I am under great affliction at hearing the bitterest reproaches uttered against you, for having become an advocate for those criminals who are charged with the murder of their fellow citizens. Good God! Is it possible? I will not believe it."

Young Quincy wrote his father a spirited defense of his decision. Tall and handsome, he was a fervent Liberty man, but above all an idealist. And he could afford to be reckless. He already knew he was suffering from tuberculosis, which was to cut short his brilliant career five years later. John Adams, with an established practice and a wife and three children to support, had no such motive. Nor was his temperament in the least inclined to enthusiasm. A worrier by nature, he sometimes expressed awed amazement at Sam Adams, who let the citizens of Boston pay his debts and lived "like the grasshopper" from day to day. John had always self-consciously planned his career. "The art of living," he once told Cousin Samuel, had cost him "much musing and pondering and anxiety."

Adams' morale did not improve when Cousin Samuel convened a town meeting of three thousand roaring adherents to demand the immediate expulsion of the two regiments. Lieutenant Governor Thomas Hutchinson yielded one regiment, then (literally trembling with anguish) yielded both, and the soldiers trudged through a barrage of derision to boats that took them to Castle William, far out in Boston Harbor.

Sam Adams' next move was a vigorous prosecution of a trial by newspaper. Ninety-six depositions from eyewitnesses were recorded by John Hodgson, the only shorthand writer in Boston, and solemnly sworn to before justices of the peace. They were attached to a twenty-two-page report compiled by the Boston selectmen and published and distributed throughout the province, but not in Boston. The Liberty men piously declared they did not want to prejudice anyone against the defendants.

As propaganda the book was a masterful document. The ninety-six witnesses were all but unanimous in their pro-Liberty description of the murder scene. Only one man had anything even faintly favorable to say for the soldiers, and editorial comments declared him to be a liar. The rest agreed that they were all in the streets of Boston that night on utterly peaceful errands —visiting friends, attending church meetings—when they were attacked by soldiers armed with bayonets, swords, and cutlasses.

But Samuel Adams was not the only person interested in compiling a version of what happened on the night of March 5. In New York, General Thomas Gage, commander in chief of all British troops in North America, wrote to Lieutenant Colonel Dalrymple, the commander of the Boston garrison.

It is absolutely necessary everything relating to the unhappy affair of the 5th of March should appear as full as it is possible upon Captain Preston's tryal. Not only what happened on the said night should be circumstantially made to appear, but also every insult and attack made upon the troops previous thereto with the pains taken by the military to prevent quarrels between the soldiers and inhabitants. If such things cannot be introduced at the tryal, affidavits should, however, be procured of these several circumstances and printed with the tryal which ought to be taken down for the purpose. . . .

Thus from the very start the trial became far more than a matter of determining the guilt or innocence of the arrested soldiers. The King's men were out to win a conviction against the mob-rule tactics of Samuel Adams. The Liberty men were as fiercely determined to pillory Parliament's use of armed force to suppress their political rights.

Between these two bitter, determined groups of men

CONTINUED ON PAGE 102

"There's no mistake in Sam Patch!" boasted the
daring young man from Pawtucket. He was almost right. There was
one mistake—but in his line of work that was one too many

By RICHARD M. DORSON

*This illustration and those that follow are reproductions of pages from
a children's book published some forty years after Sam's untimely
death. By that time folklore had taken over completely from fact.*

Sam Patch was his name. He was born on a Massachusetts farm in the first decade of the nineteenth century, a time when a boy of modest origins had many new avenues open to him. Sam chose a very new one indeed: he jumped off waterfalls—and into American legend. There he joined the slangy, brawling, boastful heroes of Jacksonian America, sons of the western woods and the city slums: men like Davy Crockett and Mike Fink.

He began simply enough. As a boy he went to Pawtucket, Rhode Island, and found work as a mule-spinner, tending the machine that twisted and wound cotton thread in Samuel Slater's cotton mill. The mill stood just above the Pawtucket Falls, and some of the hardier mill hands used to jump into the river from the top rail of the bridge that spanned the falls, or from the roofs of adjacent mills that towered one hundred feet above the deep water. Thus Sam Patch found his career, jumping the Pawtucket Falls before admiring townspeople.

On reaching manhood, Sam went into cotton manufacturing for himself. But when his partner skipped off with the firm's funds, Patch left Rhode Island and found a job in the Hamilton cotton mills in Passaic, New Jersey. Here he made his first public jump to be reported in the newspapers (September 30, 1827), when a covered bridge was being laid across the scenic Passaic Falls. Dodging town constables, Sam appeared by a whitened oak at the edge of the precipice, just as a rolling-pin slid from the guide ropes into the chasm, leaving the bridge teetering precariously halfway across. Sam jumped the falls, swam to the pin, took the trailing rope in his mouth, and returned to shore. The pin was placed in position on the guide ropes and the bridge was successfully pulled across the gap.

The publicity given this feat set Sam to jumping before fascinated crowds throughout New York and New Jersey. On August 11, 1828, at Hoboken, he jumped ninety feet into the Hudson River from a platform erected on the masthead of a sloop. Five hundred spectators lined the shore.

A year later, a group of Buffalo citizens invited Sam to jump over Niagara Falls as an added attraction to the blasting of Table Rock, which overhung the falls from the Canadian bank. Sam missed the appointed day, but distributed the following poster after reaching Buffalo:

"TO THE LADIES AND GENTLEMEN OF WESTERN NEW-YORK AND OF UPPER CANADA
All I have to say is, that I arrived at the Falls too late, to give you a specimen of my Jumping Qualities, on the 6th inst.; but on Wednesday, I thought I would venture a small Leap, which I accordingly made, of Eighty Feet, merely to convince those that remained to see me, with what safety and ease I could descend and that I was the TRUE SAM PATCH, and to show that Some Things could be Done as well as Others; which was denied before I made the Jump. . . .

I shall, Ladies and Gentlemen, on Saturday next, Oct. 17th, precisely at 3 o'clock, P.M., leap at the FALLS OF NIAGARA, from a height of 120 to 130 feet (being 40 to 50 feet higher than I leapt before), into the eddy below. On my way down from Buffalo, on the morning of that day, in the Steam-Boat Niagara, I shall, for the amusement of the Ladies, doff my coat and Spring from the Mast head into the Niagara River.

Sam Patch of Passaic Falls, New Jersey
Buffalo, Oct. 12, 1829."

On the appointed Saturday, in a pouring rain, Sam boldly climbed a ladder to the platform, which had been built from four trees spliced together and fastened by ropes running back upon Goat Island. Before ascending, he shed his shoes and coat and tied a handkerchief about his neck. Ignoring tearful farewells and protestations from persons at the foot of the ladder, he mounted the narrow, swaying platform, which was barely large enough for a man to sit upon. Then, while the spectators cheered, he spent ten minutes displaying his poise and testing the platform. At length he rose upright, took the handkerchief from his neck and tied it about his waist, waved his hand, kissed an American flag that was flying from the platform, and stepped off, plummeting toward the swirling flood.

A general cry of "He's dead! He's lost!" swept through the crowd, according to one account; a second speaks of a benumbed silence, broken only by joyous congratulations when Sam's head burst from the waters. While handkerchiefs waved and huzzas roared, the Jumping Hero swam briskly to the shore to inform the first onrushing admirer, "There's no mistake in Sam Patch!"

Flushed with success, Sam next turned to the Genesee Falls, at Rochester, for a new conquest. By now the newspapers of the nation were playing him up, and he had acquired a group of sponsors who urged him on to still greater feats. At the top of the Genesee Falls a twenty-five-foot scaffold was erected, to lengthen the jump to a distance of 125 feet. In posters Sam announced with unwitting irony, "SAM'S LAST JUMP. SOME THINGS CAN BE DONE AS WELL AS OTHERS. THERE IS NO MISTAKE IN SAM PATCH."

Friday, the thirteenth of November, was the day Sam chose. Schooners and coaches ran excursions to the falls, and both banks swarmed with the curious, while in the saloons of Rochester betting ran high. When Sam walked out onto the grassy, tree-covered rock dividing the greater and lesser branches of the cataract, and climbed to the platform, some spectators thought he staggered and lacked his usual aplomb. Some asserted afterward that the jumper was reeling drunk; others denied that he had taken more than a glass of brandy. Sam made a brief speech: Napoleon was a great man and had conquered nations; Wellington was greater and had conquered Napoleon; but neither could jump the Genesee Falls—that was left for Sam to do.

Then he jumped. But this time the descent lacked its

TEXT CONTINUED ON PAGE 18

WONDERFUL LEAPS OF SAM PATCH.

COME, and hear the story told,
Of the feats of Sam the Bold.

All the heroes ever seen—
Heroes fat, and heroes lean;
Heroes big, and heroes small,
Heroes short, and heroes tall!
Heroes light, and heroes light,
Heroes black, and heroes white,
Up from General Thumb, the plucky,
To the Giant of Kentucky,
Were not fit to hold a match
To our hero, Sammy Patch!

See his genius budding wild,
Even as a little child,

When he turned a bold "flip-flap"
From his frightened mother's lap;
And she thought her darling boy,
Had ended there her hope and joy.

Soon of courage he gave proof,
Jumping from the hen-house roof;
Frightened hens cried, "Cluck! cluck! cluck!"
"Quack! quack! quack!" screamed goose and duck.
"Stop! stop! stop!" his mother cried,
"'Tis too late!" bold Sam replied.
Down he jumped, with deadly whack,
On the screeching gander's back.
"Safe!" the mother cried with joy;
"Goose for dinner!" said the boy.

As our hero older grew,
He became more reckless too,
'Till his friends were all dismayed
At the boldness he displayed;
And their hearts gave many a thump
As they saw each break-neck jump.
Broad-leafed tables, high-backed chairs,
Lofty windows, steep-stepped stairs,
High house-eaves, and chimneys tall—
Sammy dared and jumped them all.

Sammy, on a summer's day,
Saw his father pitching hay;
"Cricky!" cried the wondrous lad,
"Now, I'll have a joke on Dad!"
Like a weazel, sly and soft,
Up he crept into the loft,
And thrust his body through the hay,
To his father's great dismay!
Loudly rose the old man's call:
"Back, you rascal, or you'll fall!
Get you down, this nonsense check,
Or you'll surely break your neck!"
Sammy, at his father's fear
Gently smiled from ear to ear.

Leaped down "like a little man,"
Loudly laughed, and homeward ran.

Sammy soon at jumps like those,
Turned his bold, ambitious nose.
He had climbed and floundered down,
From the highest points in town,
And his heart burned with desire,
To accomplish something higher.
One bright morn the wondering people
Saw him climb the lofty steeple;
Hundreds watched him with affright,
Scaling up the dizzy height.
Past him, from the lower slats,
Whirred and buzzed the startled bats;
Round his head with hoots and howls.
Sailed the melancholy owls;
'Till, a speck against the sky,
Down he called, "How's this for high?"
Owls cried out, "Too-whit! Too-whoo!"
People cheered, "Hurrah! Halloo!"
Through the air, in swift descent,
Earthward, daring Sammy went
Squarely lighting on his feet,
In the middle of the street!

Then the people, thunder-struck
By such wondrous nerve and pluck,
With loud cheer and joyous roar,
Homeward, dauntless Sammy bore:
And his mother cried with joy
As she hugged her fearless boy;
"Oh, I was a silly mammy
Ever to have named you 'Sammy,'
For your title—kiss me—(*smack*)
Surely should be 'Jumping Jack!'"

Making all the people stare
'Round the flag-staff in the square,
Jumping in his jolly way,
From the ships' masts in the bay;
Through the land, from side to side,
Sammy's fame spread far and wide.

From all quarters (such is fame),
Pressing invitations came;
Multitudes would rush and jam
Just to get a sight of Sam.
Proud folks prouder felt to catch
By the hand, immortal Patch.

Now, amongst the many calls
One there came from Trenton Falls;
A challenge daring Sam, in fact,
To leap the roaring cataract.
What the boys would call a "stump,"
For no one thought he'd dare to jump,
But, stout of heart, on victory bent,
Prompt at the call, Sam thither went.
The spot was reached, the leap was made,
Sam tumbled down each wild cascade.

And, when his sprawling made them laugh,
He coolly said, "Oh, save your chaff!
If Trenton's crooked, you just wait,
I'll show you where I'll do it straight."

Next, to Niagara thousands flock,
To see him jump from Table Rock,
Into those waters, thunder-hurled,
The seventh wonder of the world.
Folks swarmed on bank and giddy ledge,
On dangerous precipice's edge,
Nay, really, it has been said
They stood one on the other's head,
To get a view when gallant Sam,
Came cool (and modest as a clam),
Pausing upon the trembling verge
To list to what might prove his dirge!

The sun was red, the cliffs aglow,
And foaming white the gulf below,
As Sammy turned his fearless eye
From crowded earth to brilliant sky,
And boldly took the fearful leap
Down, down, into the seething deep!

Each breath was held, each eye was
    strained—
Huzzah! at last the bank he's gained!
A shake, a gasp, his breath to catch—
"Now! who will laugh at Samuel
    Patch?"

'T was there Sam made his greatest
    dive—
Feet—full one hundred and sixty-five!

Sam's reputation loudly rings
Now, even in the courts of kings;
A world-wide pet, on flattery fed,
What wonder that it turned his head!
And after such a sad mishap,
Why marvel that *he* turned his map
When he was practising the way,
To jump to Massachusetts Bay?

But greater things were coming up
To overflow Sam's brimming cup.
A call from Washington was sent
For him to see the President!
Sam didn't care a rap at all—
He only answered, "Capitol!" (*capital*)
But when to Washington he comes
Amid the sound of trumps and drums,
And bears the rushing, crushing crowd,
All hailing him with clamor loud;
Men of all nations on the earth,
The poor man and the man of worth,
With heart fast beating, eyes aflame—
"Ha, Sam!" he cries, "this, this! is fame!"
And when, the first reception through,
Sam rigged himself—red, white, and blue—

And bade farewell to folks below,
And upward went with a "Yo! heave! ho!"
He cried out there, with a great salaam,
"Kind people, I'm the same old Sam!
But I'm going to jump across the sea,
To have a royal little spree,
So keep your eyes on this lordly dome
'Till Samuel Patch, Esquire, comes home!"
Then off, with a bounce and a spring, he flew,
O'er the heaving sea like a swift curlew,
And reached, in the space of one little hour,
The topmost peak of Windsor Tower.
His time was short, and he gobbled quick
A royal lunch with Good Queen Vic.
Then to Washington he jumped right back,
But, in his absence—what a rack!!!

Alas! that lunch with England's Queen
(A thing that never should have been),
Had, even by that short delay,
Brought change that well might cause dismay;
For, as Sam Patch back homeward leapt,
With anxious eyes the coast he swept,
In search of stately Washington,
But stately city there was none.
Drifts, heaps and hillocks, large and small,
Lay where was once the capital,
And men with wagon, cart, and dray,
Were busy clearing them away!
Astonished, Sam lit on a hump,
And closed his transatlantic jump;
And gazing 'round with interest strange,
Much marveled what had wrought this change.

The multitude had been so great
From Province, Territory, State,
That when they lunched, while Sam was gone,
'T was like a hail-storm coming on;
Or sand-waves, when the tempests tear a-
Cross the Desert of Sahara!
Sam sees that all around him lies
Remains of muffins, buns and pies,
And several mountain heaps he finds
Are wholly formed of melon-rinds;
While apple-cores and peanut-shells,
Banana-peels and what not else,
Are piled in ridge, and drift, and row,
And hide the city far below;
The summit of the dome scarce keeps
Its head above the smothering heaps.

usual arrowy precision. One third of the way down, Sam's body began to droop, his arms parted from his sides, he lost command of his body, and he struck the water obliquely with arms and legs extended. The horror-stricken assemblage waited, but he did not reappear. Dragging for the body proved unsuccessful; it was not found until the following March 17, when a farmer at the mouth of the Genesee near Lake Ontario broke the ice to water his horses.

What manner of man was he? Some called him an ignorant loafer; others idealized him as an intrepid, debonair acrobat whose next objective would have been London Bridge; still others characterized him as a devoted son (before his last leap Sam had stipulated that if he died, all proceeds should go to his mother). Whatever his actual traits, they speedily disappeared before the onrush of myth. Newspaper editors praised Sam's selfless heroism, and ministers preached sermons against his vanity and folly. Some punster composed an epitaph filled with such double meanings as *"divers* times," *"a drop too much," "untimely bier,"* and *"this sad fall,"* and concluding: *There's none alive will ever match him—/Ah, cruel Death, thus to dis-*PATCH *him!*

Many refused to believe that Sam had really died. One view held that, while practicing, Sam had discovered an eddy running under a shelving rock, and had there hidden a suit of clothes, a bottle of spirits, and some food. Following his last jump (so the story went), he had swum to this spot, remained there until dark, and had then set off incognito. A man in Albany said he had seen and talked with him; another in Rochester bet one hundred dollars that Sam would reappear in that city before the first of January; a notice posted prominently in Rochester stated that Patch would recount his adventures at Acker's Eagle Tavern during the forenoon of December 3; reports spread that he had been seen at Pittsford, Canandaigua, and other places, on his way to New Jersey. One widely printed newspaper story, signed "Sam Patch," declared the Genesee jump to be a capital hoax, with a man of straw, paint, sand, and stones having substituted for the Jumping Hero.

Even after the body was found, the stories continued; there were those who at twilight perceived Sam sporting at the falls and repeating his fearful feat to a concourse of water birds and fish.

To American poets and rhymesters of the 1830's, searching for native themes, the heroics, tragedy, and seriocomic aspects of the Last Leap proved magnetic. One poem called Sam *The Great Descender, mighty* PATCH / *Spurner of heights—great Nature's overmatch!* and unblushingly likened him to Columbus, Franklin, Newton, and Nelson.

Another account, this time in prose, has the Jumping Hero sighted in the South Seas by a Yankee whaler. Amazed, the Yankee captain asks him, "Why, Sam, how *on airth* did you get here? I thought you was drowned at the Canadian lines." "Why," says Sam, "I didn't get *on earth* here at all,

but I came slap *through* it. In that Niagara dive I went so everlasting deep, I thought it was just as short to come up t'other side, so out I came in these parts."

A spurious autobiography told Sam's life story: At the age of six months, he had leaped from Nanny's arms into a washtub of soapsuds; as a boy he was attracted to leap-frog; in school he would always skip over hard words; before he was four and a half feet tall he had jumped from the masthead of a pirogue into Hell Gate; at Niagara he had bobbed about in the froth like a huckleberry on top of a pail of freshly-drawn beer. The moral of this story was "Look before you leap."

In 1836, in Buffalo, a comedian named Dan Marble, already known for his Yankee roles, portrayed Sam Patch and found himself heir to the fame bestowed on the original. Year after year, before enthusiastic audiences in western cities, and then in New York and Boston, he played in *Sam Patch, or The Daring Yankee,* and its sequel, *Sam Patch in France, or The Pesky Snake.* The climax of the first play was Marble's leap from the flies; plummeting from a height variously estimated at between forty and seventy feet, he bobbed up triumphantly in a pool of spray and foam. Actually, Marble didn't land in water at all, but on a spring bed piled with bags of shavings, which was concealed behind the phony pool. The jumping mania affected the audiences: as Constance Rourke has written, clerks jumped counters, farmers jumped fences, boys and old folks vied in "doing Sam Patch."

The tale of Patch even became a subject for literary reference. Nathaniel Hawthorne—always receptive to American legends, particularly somber ones—was stirred when he viewed the Genesee Falls at dusk. "How stern a moral may be drawn from the story of poor Sam Patch!" he wrote. "Was the leaper of cataracts more mad or foolish than other men who throw away life, or misspend it in pursuit of empty fame and seldom so triumphantly as he?" William Dean Howells, in his novel *Their Wedding Journey,* has the hero express dismay because his young wife has never heard of Patch: "Isabel, your ignorance of all that an American woman should be proud of distresses me." As recently as 1946, the distinguished poet William Carlos Williams, in Volume I of his long poem *Paterson,* described Sam's Passaic Falls plunge.

By mid-nineteenth century, the interest in Patch had waned, but he never completely disappeared from view. Those communities with a claim to him—Pawtucket, Paterson, and especially Rochester—continued to remember him in feature articles and holiday floats. And on November 12, 1948, 119 years almost to the day after the Last Leap, Sam Patch's grave in Rochester received, by public subscription, a handsome granite marker and plaque.

Richard M. Dorson is chairman of the folklore program at the University of Indiana, Bloomington.

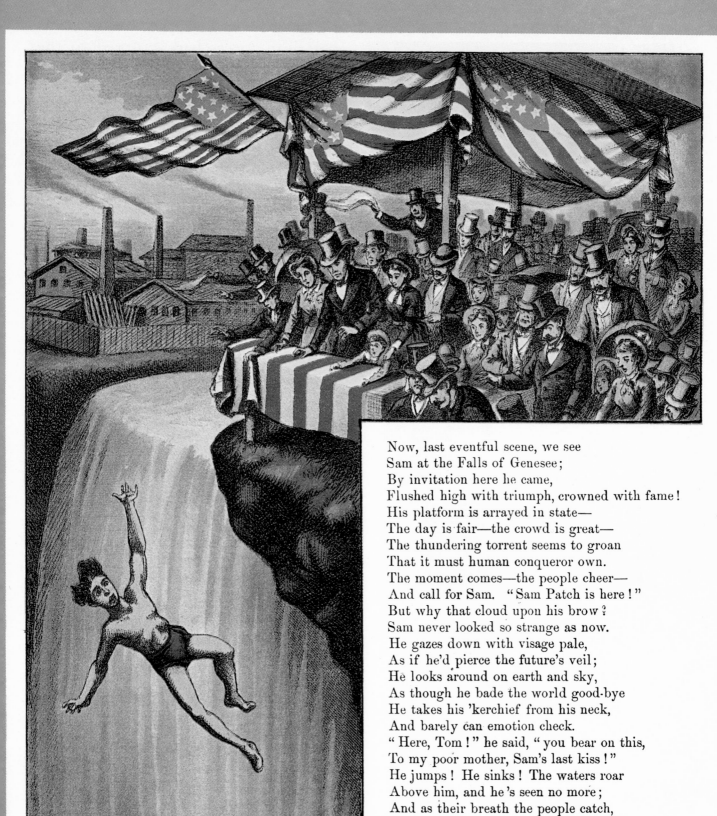

Now, last eventful scene, we see
Sam at the Falls of Genesee;
By invitation here he came,
Flushed high with triumph, crowned with fame!
His platform is arrayed in state—
The day is fair—the crowd is great—
The thundering torrent seems to groan
That it must human conqueror own.
The moment comes—the people cheer—
And call for Sam. "Sam Patch is here!"
But why that cloud upon his brow?
Sam never looked so strange as now.
He gazes down with visage pale,
As if he'd pierce the future's veil;
He looks around on earth and sky,
As though he bade the world good-bye
He takes his 'kerchief from his neck,
And barely can emotion check.
"Here, Tom!" he said, "you bear on this,
To my poor mother, Sam's last kiss!"
He jumps! He sinks! The waters roar
Above him, and he's seen no more;
And as their breath the people catch,
They sigh, "*Alas! brave, foolish Patch!*"

Rear Admiral Clifton A. F. Sprague, commander of Taffy 3

American forces had returned to the Philippines, and the Japanese Navy was about to make its last, desperate attempt to stave off defeat. Suddenly, by miscalculation, nothing stood between its most powerful task force and the American beachhead at Leyte Gulf but a small group of U.S. escort carriers. Could little Taffy 3 hold off Admiral Kurita's gigantic battleships?

THE BATTLE

Wednesday, October 25, 1944—a gloomy overcast punctuated by rain squalls gave the predawn sky a dirty yellow-gray hue. Six small United States carriers and seven escort ships moved through the somber seas east of the Philippine island of Samar. From the gently swaying flight decks of the carriers, white-starred planes took off on routine early-morning missions.

On the bridge of the flagship, U.S.S. *Fanshaw Bay*, Rear Admiral Clifton A. F. Sprague watched the Grumman aircraft rise into the northeasterly wind toward the broken ceiling of clouds. The day had all the earmarks of being another long, tiresome succession of reconnaissance, antisubmarine, and ground-support missions. Sprague, a forty-eight-year-old veteran, scanned his little fleet, called Taffy 3 (its radio call sign). Merchant-ship hulls turned into baby flattops to meet wartime needs, the thin-skinned escort carriers—designated CVE's—were not even half the size of conventional aircraft carriers. Old hands claimed the CVE stood for "Combustible, Vulnerable, Expendable." Three destroyers and four destroyer escorts ringed the flotilla of CVE's like watchful guard dogs. Somewhere to the south, Sprague knew, two other carrier groups, Taffies 1 and 2, were on similar missions in support of the American G.I.'s who had gone ashore at Leyte Gulf five days earlier. Together the three Taffies made

up Escort Carrier Task Group 77.4 of the United States Seventh Fleet.

The first warning of a break in the morning routine came shortly after six thirty as the ships' crews sat down to breakfast. Radio equipment in the *Fanshaw Bay*'s Combat Information Center picked up Japanese voices. Since the nearest enemy ships were supposedly over a hundred miles away, the American radiomen reasoned that the enemy chatter must be coming from one of the nearby Japanese-held islands. With the exception of the beachhead on Leyte and a few islands in the adjacent gulf, all of the Philippine archipelago was in Japanese hands.

Eleven minutes later, a message flashed in from an American scout plane. The unbelievable words were hurriedly relayed to the bridge: "Enemy surface force . . . twenty miles northwest of your task group and closing at 30 knots."

Admiral Sprague, at this moment, was trying to make sense of two other odd reports. His lookouts had just seen antiaircraft fire on the northern horizon, and his radar had picked up an unidentified something in the same direction. Surely, Sprague was thinking, the cause of all the unexpected commotion must be Admiral William Halsey's Third Fleet, the closest large naval unit to Taffy 3. The pilot's message stopped him short.

History of United States Naval Operations in World War II, BY SAMUEL ELIOT MORISON; COURTESY ATLANTIC-LITTLE, BROWN

Commander Dwight C. Shepler, U.S.N.R., painted this eye-witness view of U.S. destroyers in action off Samar.

OFF SAMAR By WILFRED P. DEAC

"Check that identification!" ordered Sprague, hoping with a growing feeling of doubt that some innocent mistake had been made by the scout plane. But confirmation came from another source—a lookout on one of Sprague's other carriers, the *Kitkun Bay.* Scanning the horizon beneath the gradually clearing cumulus cloud canopy, the seaman could make out pagodalike masts: Japanese battleships and cruisers.

Admiral Sprague's voice boomed into the squawk box: "Come to course 090 degrees . . . launch all planes as soon as possible . . . speed 16."

The little carriers swung due east, far enough into the wind to launch aircraft without bringing them closer to the enemy. Planes were soon soaring into the damp sky armed with whatever bombs and bullets they had when the alarm sounded. Gun crews settled expectantly behind the breeches of the carriers' 5-inch guns—the biggest they had.

At 6:58 A.M., bright flashes lit the horizon seventeen miles north of the flotilla. Sixty seconds later, Japanese range-marker shells rattled into the sea to throw towering geysers of colored water into the air behind the American carriers. The Battle off Samar had begun.

The Battle off Samar was a direct result of Japanese High Command plans. As the American forces advanced relentlessly across the Southern Pacific during the final months of World War II, four *Sho*

(Conquer) plans were devised to blunt U.S. thrusts against the Empire's inner defenses. At best, these were little more than delaying tactics which might postpone the end of the war and give Japan a better bargaining position at the peace table. Sho No. 1 was designed to counter any United States move against the Philippine Islands, and by the fall of 1944, with the Americans moving northwestward, it appeared that the time for putting it into effect had arrived.

In mid-October the Imperial Japanese Navy began to move. Powerful naval forces steamed eastward from the Lingga Archipelago near Singapore, and southward from the home islands. On October 18, while the Japanese fleets were still at sea, the word flashed from Combined Fleet commander Admiral Soemu Toyoda in Tokyo: "Execute Sho Plan No. 1!" American landings had begun in Leyte Gulf, in the east-central Philippines.

Two U.S. fleets were covering the invasion beaches —the Third Fleet, under Admiral William F. Halsey, composed mainly of fast new battleships and big carriers; and the Seventh Fleet, commanded by Vice Admiral Thomas C. Kinkaid, made up mostly of pre-Pearl Harbor battlewagons and cruisers. The Third Fleet was acting the role of roving watchdog, while the Seventh was directly overseeing the landing of Sixth Army G.I.'s on Leyte Island.

Sho Plan No. 1 was to be a three-pronged maneuver supported by land-based aircraft. A Northern Force under Vice Admiral Jisaburo Ozawa would steam southward from Japan and attempt to decoy away the protecting American Third Fleet. This Japanese force was made up of four regular carriers, two converted battleship-carriers, and smaller screening vessels. The battleship-carriers—the *Ise* and the *Hyuga*—were merely old battleships with their two main aft turrets replaced by small flight decks. Designed to compensate for Japan's shortage of aircraft carriers, the hybrid ships would never have a chance to prove themselves. There were not enough airplanes available in the fall of 1944 to give the *Ise* and the *Hyuga* even one of the twenty-four each was supposed to carry; and Ozawa's other carriers were decidedly short of planes, too.

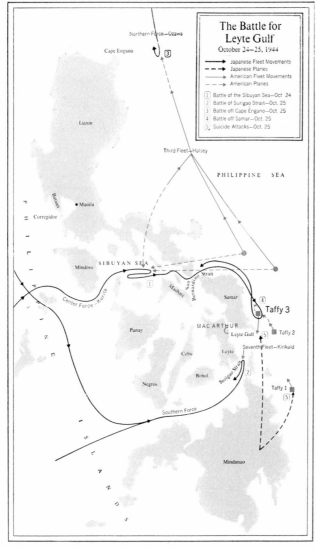

As the legend on this map indicates, the Battle off Samar was one action in the Battle for Leyte Gulf—often said to have been the greatest sea fight in all of naval history.

The second prong of Sho No. 1 was to swing in against the Americans in Leyte Gulf from the southwest, through Surigao Strait. The mélange of battleships, cruisers, and destroyers in this Southern Force—seventeen ships in all—were commanded by Vice Admirals Kiyohide Shima and Shoji Nishimura.

The third prong, the Center Force, was the most potent of the Nipponese units, and was to deliver the knockout blow. Sailing from Lingga Roads during the early morning hours of October 18, it would stop at North Borneo for refueling and final preparations. Then, following a devious path through the Sibuyan Sea and San Bernardino Strait north of Leyte, it would swing around and enter Leyte Gulf through "the back door"—from the east. In this key Center Force, under Vice Admiral Takeo Kurita, were the world's two largest warships, the *Yamato* and the *Musashi.* Each displaced 68,000 tons and carried 18.1-inch guns, as compared to 45,000 tons and 16-inch guns for the largest U.S. warship. Also in this formidable fleet were the battleships *Haruna, Kongo,* and *Nagato,* twelve cruisers, and fifteen destroyers.

Once inside Leyte Gulf, Shima's and Nishimura's Southern Force and Kurita's Center Force were to pool their firepower to disrupt the American invasion. Whatever lay in the gulf or blocked its approaches, warships and cargo vessels alike, was to be wiped out. The importance of Ozawa's Northern Force as a decoy to draw off the powerful U.S. Third Fleet was emphasized by the marked Japanese inferiority in aircraft and by the total number of fleet units involved—64 Nipponese vessels against 216 American and 2 Australian warships.

In undertaking Sho Plan No. 1, the Japanese were placed in the unenviable position of the frantic poker player who, reduced to a few chips after a losing streak, plays his hand all or nothing. Admiral Kurita said to his officers before the battle: "I know many of you are strongly opposed to this assignment. But the war situation is far more critical than any of you can possibly know. Would it not be a shame to have the fleet remain intact while our nation perishes? . . . You must all remember there are such things as miracles. What man can say there is no chance for our fleet to turn the tide of war in a decisive battle?"

First blow in the Battle for Leyte Gulf was struck by the U.S. submarine *Darter* against the Center Force as Kurita's ships steamed northeast along Palawan, the daggerlike island jutting southwest from the middle of the Philippine archipelago. The sub's torpedoes slammed into two of the enemy cruisers just as the first light of October 23 was streaking the eastern sky. The force flagship, the heavy cruiser *Atago,* shuddered and sank in less than twenty minutes, sending Admiral Kurita and his staff for an unscheduled swim before they were rescued by a destroyer. The cruiser *Takao,*

Japanese shells sank the United States carrier Gambier Bay *a few minutes after this picture caught four of them bursting at once.*

also hit, belched fire and smoke. The task force swung to starboard into the path of a second U.S. submarine. Torpedoes from the *Dace* scrubbed the cruiser *Maya* from the scene in four minutes. Kurita, shifting his command post to the huge *Yamato,* was badly shaken up. The enemy hadn't even been sighted, and already five valuable warships (counting two destroyers detached to escort the damaged *Takao* to Borneo) were eliminated from the battle to come.

The sun shone down from clear skies on white-capped water and mountainous islands as the Center Force moved into the Sibuyan Sea northwest of Leyte on Tuesday, October 24. Within twenty-four hours, if all went well, Kurita's ships would be steaming into Leyte Gulf from the east. But their bad luck had not left them yet. Their antiaircraft batteries, nervously anticipating American air strikes, cut loose at a flight of fighter planes soon after dawn. It was a mistake, and a costly one for the Center Force. The planes were land-based Japanese Zeros ordered to provide air cover for Kurita. Faced with heavy antiaircraft fire from the very warships they were to protect, the fighters understandably returned to their island base.

Then, at 8:10 that morning, an American scout plane sighted the Japanese armada. Two hours and sixteen minutes later, single-engined bombers and fighters from the carriers of Admiral Halsey's Third

Fleet pounced on the Center Force. Dodging the pink and purple bursts of antiaircraft fire, American Hell-divers and Avengers pressed one attack after another against the wildly weaving ships. At the cost of eighteen dive bombers and torpedo planes, they sank the gargantuan *Musashi,* badly damaged a heavy cruiser, and slightly hurt the other battleships. Kurita wavered —he actually had his fleet reverse course for several hours—but in the end he rallied and carried on toward San Bernardino Strait.

Admiral Halsey was very much pleased by his carrier pilots' reports of their successes over the Sibuyan Sea. Unfortunately, these reports were somewhat exaggerated, and led him to the optimistic conclusion that Kurita's Center Force "could no longer be considered a serious menace." Meanwhile Admiral Ozawa's decoy Northern Force had been cruising the waters of the Philippine Sea off Luzon, hoping to be spotted by Halsey's search planes. About 4 P.M. on October 24, one of the searchers made the contact, and by 8:30 that evening the whole U.S. Third Fleet was off in enthusiastic pursuit of the Japanese bait—sixty-five warships against seventeen.

It was a questionable action, and led to one of the hottest controversies about naval tactics in World War II. Halsey had enough ships and planes to handle both Ozawa and Kurita; but as it was, nobody was left to

CONTINUED ON PAGE 95

Marching on Washington is an old custom. When "General" Jacob Coxey
and his Commonweal Army approached in 1894,
the city trembled. But "the most dangerous man since the Civil War"
meekly surrendered when nabbed for walking on the grass

Rebel in a Wing Collar

By GEORGE A. GIPE

At 12:30 P.M., Easter Sunday, 1894, a band of one hundred men began slowly to march eastward out of Massillon, Ohio. The group's destination and purpose were summed up in the words of an improvised battle hymn that a few of them sang as they trudged: *We're marching on to Washington,/ To right the nation's wrongs.*

It was not a good day for singing: the weather was cold and damp, the turnout of marchers disappointingly small. The more sensitive "soldiers" felt embarrassment at the publicity they were receiving, for forty-three special newspaper correspondents representing every major daily in the East were in attendance, with four Western Union telegraph operators and two linemen. "Never in the annals of insurrection has so small a company of soldiers been accompanied by such a phalanx of recording angels," wrote the visiting British reformer William T. Stead in the *Review of Reviews.*

The column formed behind a Negro carrying an American flag; another man dressed in typical cowboy attire of buckskin jacket, wide slouch hat, pantaloons, and heavy boots; a seven-piece band; and a buggy drawn by two bay mares—the official vehicle of the army's "commanding general," Jacob S. Coxey. For many months, this gold-spectacled, dapper man in conservative business attire had sent out page after page of advance publicity, warning the nation that the plight of America's unemployed could be ignored no longer, that as many as 100,000 men would descend on Washington unless legislation were passed to provide work and food for the stricken millions.

Here, at left, in May of 1894, is Coxey, the utterly respectable rebel. With him in the police cage are Christopher Columbus Jones, a lieutenant, and (at right) Coxey's principal aide, Carl "Old Greasy" Browne, carnival barker, labor agitator, artist, and sometime seller of Kickapoo Indian Remedy.

The year 1893, the beginning of a four-year depression, had not been a good one for either employer or workingman. Farming was rapidly becoming an unreliable means of earning a living; overspeculation, tariff problems, and free-silver agitation had thrown business into chaos, with eight thousand business houses collapsing in six months—an extraordinary figure for the period. Dozens of railroads were in the hands of receivers, and Henry Adams wrote: "Business executives died like flies under the strain."

For the workingman, conditions were deplorable. Struggling with long hours and low pay, bereft of any semblance of what we nowadays call job security, workmen attempted to band together in trade unions, but soon discovered that unless they resorted to violence they were ignored. The federal government, firmly dedicated to the prevailing *laissez-faire* policy, took no steps to ease the plight of business or of labor. As a result, three million men were left unemployed during the bitter winter of 1893–94, and the number of tramps wandering the countryside was said to be more than 60,000.

Against this gloomy background emerged the black-garbed, wing-collared Massillon reformer: he was labor's champion but the enemy of violence. Jacob Sechler Coxey was born in Selinsgrove, Pennsylvania, on Easter Sunday, April 16, 1854. Educated in the public schools at Danville, he quit at fifteen to work in a steel mill. He said later that the spare hours of his youth were spent reading and thinking about the fallacies of a money system that permitted frequent economic depressions. By 1890, the thirty-six-year-old Coxey had been married twice, and had moved from his home state of Pennsylvania to Massillon, Ohio, where he operated a successful stone quarry. He was a man with no particular hobbies, a nonsmoking Episcopalian who had established himself as a respectable, wealthy, and apparently conventional businessman.

Coxey's political and economic views, however, were anything but conventional. A member of the Populist Party, formed in 1892 out of western and southern agrarian groups, with some support from labor and from reform movements, Coxey entertained Greenback and other legal-tender theories that were predictably simplistic. "There's nothing wrong with this country that money won't cure" was one of his mottoes and a clue to his rather hazy ideas of finance. Everything would be all right, Coxey believed, if the government could be induced to issue virtually unlimited amounts of paper money and use it to pay the jobless hordes to labor on public works. The money was to be secured by non-interest-bearing bonds. Understandably, after daily buggy rides over the five miles of rutty roads between Massillon and his stone quarry, Coxey selected the building of good highways as the most pressing need of the nation.

Coxey's attempts to spread these theories were not notably successful. In the summer of 1893, he tried to address a large gathering of unemployed on Chicago's lake front, only to have the meeting dispersed on orders of Mayor Carter Harrison. At the Populist convention some months later, however, he did rather better. Not only did his ideas intrigue many delegates of the reform party, but he won an introduction to a man who could put these ideas before the public. Carl Browne, whom a contemporary writer called "the flower of American demagogism" was a veteran of Denis Kearney's anti-Chinese-labor riots on the sandlots of San Francisco; he had also been a cartoonist, medicine man, orator, and organizer. No shrinking violet, Browne often wore a buckskin jacket buttoned with silver half-dollars, stamped with the word FREE. Long black hair flowed from beneath his Buffalo Bill cowboy hat, framing a round, heavily bearded face.

Carl Browne's flamboyant appearance and matching disposition brought him the dislike of many men, but Coxey found him delightful. Twenty years after their first meeting, Coxey wrote, "I can say no more here than I have said to my friends many, many times, that Browne was the most unselfish man of my entire life's acquaintance. He never gave a thought to pecuniary gain. His whole heart was in the movement to emancipate labor. . . ." Coxey's sincere admiration for Browne can hardly be doubted: he encouraged one of his young daughters to marry the former medicine man, an age difference of over twenty years notwithstanding. Together the two visionaries transformed Coxey's assortment of theories into a vital cause.

Coxey's plan had already been presented to Congress in the form of two bills providing for the creation of a country-road fund, backed by $500 million in non-interest-bearing government bonds. All of the road work was to be done by the unemployed on the basis of an eight-hour day at a $1.50 daily minimum wage. The plan not only looked to public works as relief measures, but also, in effect, would have put the federal government in direct competition with private enterprise. Yet Coxey had no illusions. "Having very little faith that Congress would do more than pigeon-hole these bills," he wrote, "the idea was conceived of presenting the demand to Congress in the form of a petition with boots on." Coxey's Army was born.

Carl Browne, although officially second in command, was the primary spokesman and publicist for the march. His design became the banner for the "Army of the Commonweal," a portrait of Christ with the slogan: "Peace on Earth, Good Will to Men, But Death to Interest on Bonds." Browne also drew up an organizational chart for the army, dividing it into "communes, regiments, and cantons," each led by a marshal. As things turned out, this was rather more than was needed, for when Coxey's legion ended its first day's march on the outskirts of Canton, Ohio, it was found to number not more than one hundred men.

Many things besides sheer impracticality dogged the footsteps of this little band. One was the effective rumor that Coxey and Browne had set themselves up as religious figures. Stead wrote that Coxey "is said to be convinced that he and Browne are between them sharers of the reincarnation of Christ." Then, as if to reassure his readers that such a claim was entirely out of the question, Stead added, "Coxey wears spectacles, is married, and has six children." But Browne did little to discourage this notion, referring to himself as the "cerebellum of Christ" and Coxey as the "cerebrum." Yet he meant to create a religious atmosphere, not found a religion. In one of his bulletins to "the troops," Browne wrote: "I believe that a part of the soul of Christ happened to come into my being by reincarnation. I believe also that another part of Christ's soul is in brother Coxey . . . I also believe that the remainder of the soul of Christ has been fully reincarnated in the thousands of people throughout the United States today, and that accounts for the tremendous response to this call of ours to try to bring about peace and plenty to take the place of panic and poverty. To accomplish it means the Second Coming of Christ, and I believe in the prophecy that He is to come, not in any single form, but in the whole people."

The soldiers themselves did not please most people who saw them pass. Many recruits were simply unemployed workmen, but the army had its seamier side. Besides Browne, who was given to ranting, there were such fellow travellers as an astrologer; the author of a pamphlet entitled *Dogs and Fleas, by One of the Dogs;*

a Cherokee Indian who was trying to live on a diet of oatmeal; a man calling himself "The Great Unknown," who was trailed by a mysterious veiled lady; a trumpet player named "Windy" Oliver; and many ordinary tramps who had seized on the march as a good way of assuring themselves of a free meal. Secretary of Agriculture J. Sterling Morton summed up the qualities of the average marcher: "Homeless . . . taxless . . . nomadic. . . . If a life history of each individual in Coxey's army could be truthfully written, it would show, no doubt, that each of them has paid out, from birth to death, more money for tobacco, whiskey and beer, than for clothing, education, taxes and food all put together."

Few contemporary accounts credited the Coxeyites with being more than a gang of tramps, but there was one reasonably objective study of 290 members of the Commonweal Army made by a professor at the University of Chicago. One half were reported as American-born, and two thirds as English-speaking. The average age was between thirty and thirty-two; 181 were skilled mechanics representing seventy trades, of whom less than half were union members. Eighty-eight professed to be Democrats; thirty-nine, Republicans; and ten, Populists; the remainder had not voted or had not yet been naturalized. One fourth of the total claimed they had needed charity to get through the preceding winter, and the average length of unemployment was five months. The study claimed that only five or six of the 290 were of "questionable" character.

Most Americans would have rejected such moderate views of the army, and many feared that this thin stream of the discontented could swell into a massive river of protest. There was much speculation about whether the movement was legal, and what might come of it if left uncontrolled. Representative Joseph Outhwaite of Ohio pleaded that "if Coxey's followers will only think, they will see that if from 10,000 to 50,000 men can intimidate Congress to do one thing, then another 10,000 to 50,000 men can intimidate them to do another thing—which leads to anarchy." Senator William Stewart of Nevada wrote a letter to Coxey urging him to "use the ballot box to protect liberty," while others professed concern that the army would starve along the way.

Coxey himself was vague when asked how he intended to feed his army. In an interview at Pittsburgh, he claimed that the army would emulate Christ by "plucking the ears of corn along the way," but he also stated that his troops were "patriots, not bummers." Actually, he hoped for donations along the route, and was not often disappointed. Police and town officials may have been hostile to his cause, but they had no desire to prod the army into riots. Most communities provided shelter by opening their jails or by setting up sanitary facilities in fields or public buildings. No

"And so they did at Washington
    when Coxey's army came,
The millionaires got out and said
    that Coxey was to blame.
For marching on the Capitol with
    such a Commonweal,
Composed of men who would not 'put
    their shoulders to the wheel.'
But when you say that there are men
    who only care to shirk,
You must get out yourself and try
    to find a little work.
With money scarce and business dull,
    and then see how you feel.
Your shoulder may be willing but
    you cannot find a wheel."

The immortal lines above are by Chesterfield W. Myers, the poet of the Commonweal. At right, the army itself passes through a Pennsylvania town.

doubt some townspeople donated food simply as a means of moving the army on its way, but there were more than a few places that welcomed the Army of the Commonweal with genuine enthusiasm. Allegheny City presented them with a new banner reading, "Laws for Americans. More money, less misery, good roads. No interest-bearing bonds." And on March 27, two days out of Massillon, the army was treated to a rousing reception at Economy, Pennsylvania, where it was given a wagonload of potatoes, bread, ginger cakes, and other food. Here and there the hat was passed, and at Cumberland, Maryland, with his men camped in the baseball park, Coxey charged the curious ten cents admission. The take was $145.

The job of disciplining the troops of the army fell to Browne, who attacked the task with such obvious enthusiasm that he was quickly dubbed "that greasy old humbug" by his men. Although he spent a good deal of time writing bulletins and haranguing capitalists, Browne did try out morale-building ideas, one of them the formal presentation of merit certificates whenever the situation was appropriate. When the army crossed the Blue Mountains in a snowstorm, one of these cards of merit was issued, a sample of which reads, "This is to certify that John Southers of Group 3, Commune 1, Chicago Community of the Commonweal of Christ, is entitled to this souvenir of heroic conduct in crossing the Cumberland Mountains in the

face of ice and snow, and despite police persecution and dissension breeders." At another time, Browne thought that some music might cheer the troops, and as they crossed the Pennsylvania border heading south, he ordered the playing of "Maryland, My Maryland."

During the first week of April, the army began to enlarge, though not as dramatically as Coxey had hoped and predicted. Passing through Homestead, Pennsylvania, the Commonweal ranks swelled from three hundred to six hundred, enough to cause a stir of apprehension in Washington. On April 18, Congress first took official recognition of the approach of Coxey's Army by staying in special session until six thirty in the evening. A show of armed force was voted down, even after a newspaper article pointed out that "L'Enfant, who had experienced the horrors of the revolution in Paris . . . laid out the city [of Washington] with the especial design of preventing a repetition of such horrors. . . . The avenues radiated from centers which could be commanded by a few Gatling guns."

By this time the "march on Washington" was something of a national movement, with contingents of unemployed ready to move out from Los Angeles, San Francisco, and Chicago. They had been independently organized, but in the public mind they were inseparably associated with Coxey, whose group got most of the national attention. Typical was the "army" of 350, under Charlie Kelly, which gathered in San

Francisco on April 3. When the mayor of San Francisco could find no way of dispersing them, he saw to it that they were given free transportation across the Bay— an act that did not endear him to the mayor of Oakland. The citizens of Oakland promptly raised enough money to hurry the army to Sacramento, but when the troops marched down to the railroad yards and saw common boxcars awaiting them instead of passenger cars, they turned around and marched back to Oakland. A general alarm was sounded, Gatling guns were wheeled in front of City Hall, the police and fire departments were armed, and 1,200 citizens were deputized, before the Commonwealers and their commander finally accepted the boxcar offer. Few of them, however, were ever to reach Washington, for their troubles on the West Coast anticipated what they would encounter all the way.

In the meantime, Coxey's own army was struggling through Maryland in the midst of a fight for power between two of his lieutenants. The discontent that bred mutiny may have erupted for any of a number of reasons, possibly because Coxey himself was off on a side trip, perhaps because Carl Browne was riding while the others were walking, and was staying in the best hotels while his men were sleeping in tents or on the floors of jails. On April 14, the man called The Great Unknown staged an uprising, and might have wrested the leadership from Browne, had Coxey not returned just in time to restore the peace. He ordered the Unknown and his lady friend out of camp. Even Coxey's son, Jesse, was purged and banished for associating with the mutineers; later he was reinstated "on condition that he not sulk anymore." After this melodrama, many correspondents who had been reporting Coxey's march in an objective manner began to do what they had wanted to do from the start—that is, burlesque it. This was hotly resented by Coxey and Browne, who attacked the writers as "argus-eyed demons of hell."

Long exasperated with the press, Coxey devised a plan to get rid of them. Hiring two Chesapeake and Ohio canalboats at Cumberland, he piled the army aboard and announced that they would travel in that way for the next hundred miles. Previously, the newspapermen had followed the army by horseback and

At Cumberland, Maryland, Coxey's army took to the Chesapeake and Ohio Canal (far left) to evade the large press corps, which had started turning in jocular reports. But the press followed on another boat until the troops disembarked. This photograph shows the army's banner, painted by Browne: a portrait of Christ (which bears some resemblance to the artist). Browne himself, with his half-dollar buttons and cowboy hat, stands to the right of the banner. At left, Coxey, in his command buggy, leads on toward Washington.

carriage, and had taken turns tagging along on foot. Now they could not bear to let the army sail away from them, so they rented a third canalboat for pursuit. A cook and ample supplies of food and drink were rounded up, and the vessel was christened the *Flying Demon,* after Browne's hot words. From her deck, reporters sent back entertaining descriptions of the newly amphibious army. "It was like a floating picture of Victor Hugo," one correspondent wrote, ". . . the ragged forms swarming like rats over every foot of the craft, and rough . . . faces . . . peering through the cabin windows like the victims of the old French galleys."

The cruise of the *Flying Demon* came to an end at Williamsport, Maryland, where Coxey and his army took to the road again. Just outside of Washington they paused to await the arrival of a contingent from Philadelphia under the leadership of "Marshal" Christopher Columbus Jones—a force which amounted to eighteen men, an American flag, and a bulldog. On the day Jones arrived, April 23, the District of Columbia commissioners issued a manifesto directed at the Coxeyites, forbidding the soliciting of funds in the capital and warning them against assembling on the grounds of the Capitol building or obstructing public roads or highways. Chief of Police William G. Moore announced that he intended to arrest Coxey if he moved into the city, citing an 1830 law that made it a penal offense to bring any person into Washington who was likely to become a public charge. Then the Commonweal Army and the constabulary paused, each waiting for the other to make the first move.

Unfortunately for Coxey, this was the moment when first blood was spilled in what until then had been a remarkably peaceful movement. Some portions of the western contingents had been appropriating boxcars as a means of transportation; and when a group of "Coxeyites" started to make off with a Northern Pacific Railway car at Butte, Montana, a pitched battle ensued, with each side suffering one casualty. President Cleveland quickly sent federal troops to Butte, with orders to arrest the leaders of "the mob" and bring them to trial. Public sentiment for Coxey, whatever there was of it, quickly dissipated. Nevertheless, he chose to carry on. "I dare the police to arrest my men!" he replied to the suggestion that there might be violent action; and to the suggestion that there might be complete inaction, "If they starve in the streets of Washington, the stench from their ashes will force Congressional relief."

On May 1, 1894, thousands of spectators gathered along Pennsylvania Avenue to witness the arrival of Coxey's army in downtown Washington. "Such a fantastic aggregation never paraded itself in seriousness

CONTINUED ON PAGE 101

The Trotter

By PETER C. WELSH

The date was October 21, 1831. The place was Philadelphia's Hunting Park. The contest consisted of four three-mile heats, under saddle, for a purse of $300. R. S. Hillman captured it all in this earliest-known painting of an American trotting race.

At a flying clip the trotting horse moved effortlessly through the nineteenth century, easily distancing all competitors as the country's most widely acclaimed hero of sport. In lesser circumstances he pulled a sleigh, a road wagon, or a plow. He was a dashing symbol for a nation that liked its pleasures to have a practical aura. The trotter was a favorite of the printmakers, and their portraits of him on the track, on the road, in the solitary splendor of his stall, or in a quiet pasture brightened walls of homes, hotels, offices, and livery stables.

He had been a long time reaching the perfection he attained in the nineteenth century. The ancients, both Greeks and Romans, undoubtedly trained some horses to trot consistently—that is, to move a foreleg on one side and a hind leg on the other at the same time. This gait greatly increased the smoothness and endurance with which a horse could pull a chariot or wagon. Trotting matches were popular in many parts of the Old World, and the term "trotters," derived from a French word meaning "to tread," was in use in the sixteenth century.

Trotters came to Virginia and New England almost with the first Englishmen, though the Puritan ministers of the north frowned upon all horse racing. But in the late eighteenth and early nineteenth centuries, when the advantages of a good trotter under saddle or pulling a buggy dawned on the circuit-riding parsons, their opposition rapidly declined. As a result ministerial tirades were seldom hurled against the harness races at the state and county fairs that were so much a part of the nineteenth-century American scene. The unutilitarian flat racers never got any such seal of approval.

Early in the 1850's, a writer surveyed the country's equestrian scene and observed that the breeding, training, and racing of trotting horses was "the people's sport, the people's pastime and, consequently, is, and will be supported by the people." Currier and Ives, best-known of the nineteenth-century lithographers, at an early date billed themselves as publishers of "Colored Engravings for the People," a sobriquet applicable to most American printmakers. It is little wonder that the lithograph—already the medium of popular art—reflected the nation's favorite sporting pursuit. Only town views outnumbered horse portraits, track scenes, and views of trotters on the road among subjects in the commercial lithographer's repertory.

Everyone—tradesman, artisan, businessman, farmer, clergyman, doctor, mechanic—whose affairs required the services of a horse kept "a fast and hardy trotter." By the 1830's, north and east of the Mason-Dixon Line, it was not, according to the writer Frank Forester, unusual in a day's time in any rural district to see "a hundred persons travelling in light wagons, sulkies, or chaises, for five—I hardly think I should err, if I were to say for one—on horseback."

In the selection of a roadster, as the fast trotters were called, even the most style-conscious buyer had a wide latitude. Some owners liked a horse that was round and smooth, with soft hair, fine coloring, and a proud, showy style—one not too fast or endowed with any great endurance, but an animal that might attract the admiration of their neighbors. Color was a serious criterion to many horse owners. White, light sorrel, cream-colored, and spotted horses were objectionable; bays, chestnuts, blacks, and dark browns were the rage.

Men of means such as William H. Vanderbilt adopted the trotter and made his perfection an avocation. Robert Bonner, owner of the New York *Ledger,* and proprietor of a marvelous stud farm and stables at Tarrytown, at one time or another owned most of the champion trotters of the last half of the nineteenth century, among them Dexter, Rarus, Lady Palmer, and Flatbush Maid. Boston's Brighton Road, where the boys were "wont to exercise their fast nags," and New York's Harlem Lane, which enjoyed "a wide reputation with the lovers of the turf," were most frequently pictured and perhaps best known. Then there was Philadelphia's Rope Ferry Road, the popular thoroughfare to Point Breeze Park and the races. These scenes in the

31

big cities were simply projections on a larger scale of the stylish prancing visible in towns and hamlets throughout the country.

The road offered special pleasures in winter. Hiram Woodruff wrote nostalgically of the 1840's and of "sleigh-riding, when the air is keen and frosty, the sky clear, the snow deep and crisp." But by 1868 in New York City the sound of sleigh bells and the crunch of snow under a trotter's hoofs had largely disappeared. "The street railroads," wrote Woodruff, speaking of the horsecars, "have done for all that." In country towns and villages, however, the road in winter remained the delight so often seen in lithographic views. The Boston winter scenes by Haskell & Allen of the Fearnaught Stallions and of the mélange of sleighs leaving Brighton for the Mill-Dam prove to any eye that trotters, toddies, and Albany cutters were an exhilarating combination.

In the veins of the trotting horse so essential to this scene mingled the blood of English thoroughbreds and of sturdy American mares. The quality of the stock was improved by the sound crossbreeding of proven track performers. The stallion Messenger arrived in Philadelphia from England in 1788 and was a fountainhead of American trotters. The turf favorites of a century—Lady Suffolk, Dexter, Goldsmith Maid, Flora Temple—all had a trace of Messenger blood, as did William Rysdyk's prodigious stallion, Hambletonian. The famous New England breed of Morgan horses was founded at the end of the eighteenth century with a stallion owned by one Justin Morgan, a schoolteacher from Randolph Center, Vermont. By mid-nineteenth century no breed of horse was more popular or sought after, and such Morgan stalwarts as Ethan Allen and Black Hawk added to the luster of the tribe. Bellfounder (imported by James Root of Boston in 1823), the Canadians (derived from French stock), and the Copper Bottoms of Kentucky and the Middle West were but a few of the individual horses and strains which strengthened American trotting.

At first trotters raced "under saddle," but were later harnessed to a high four-wheeled wagon or a two-wheeled sulky, and, at last, exclusively, "to the bike sulky." The best horses were, as a rule, six seconds slower for the mile when hitched to wagons than a trotter under saddle, and three seconds slower for that distance when harnessed to a sulky. Owners and breeders struggled to trot the mile in two minutes or under, and prized the stamina that permitted a horse to go the distance through several heats.

In the 1850's, trotting matches dominated agricultural fairs, and racing meetings provided a lively interest for all levels of society from April through

TEXT CONTINUED ON PAGE 49

A Trotting Portfolio

The lithographs on the sixteen pages beginning at right are from the Harry T. Peters America on Stone Lithography *Collection in the Smithsonian Institution, consisting of some 1,700 prints, predominantly non-Currier & Ives. The collection was given by the Peters family in 1960. Below are captions giving information not found on the lithographs themselves.*
HARTFORD RACES: *The track depicted on this poster, the only print in our portfolio by Currier & Ives, is not Charter Oak Park in Hartford, Connecticut. The scene was a standard view often used for track advertising.*
COLUMBUS AND SALLY MILLER: *Columbus was an outstanding trotter who won some twenty-two purses and matches. Though the lithograph by George Endicott of New York shows him as black, he was a bright bay. Trotters raced under saddle regularly until the 1850's.*
SMUGGLER: *This lithograph was published by Haskell & Allen of Boston, second only to Currier & Ives in the number and quality of their trotting prints. Smuggler, a western "import," was foaled in Ohio in 1866 and trained in Leavenworth, Kansas. He was bought by Colonel H. S. Russell of Milton, Massachusetts, for more than thirty thousand dollars.*
BEST TIME ON RECORD: *In this print of the great trot at East Saginaw, Michigan, the captions identifying the horses are reversed. Goldsmith Maid is the horse on the inside, while the blaze-faced horse is Judge Fullerton. The lithographer is unknown.*
TROTTING CRACKS OF PHILADELPHIA: *Point Breeze Park, a famous trotting spot near the Schuylkill River, was completed in 1855. H. Pharazyn of Philadelphia issued this print in 1870.*
FEARNAUGHT STALLIONS: *David Nevins' great stallions were the scourge of the Mill-Dam, where Boston turfmen frequently held their "trials of speed."*
LEAVING BRIGHTON HOTEL FOR THE MILL-DAM: *The Mill-Dam was a favorite trotting ground for Bostonians both winter and summer until the turn of the century.*
RARUS: *In a fast decade, Rarus's record made in Buffalo in 1878 stood for less than a year. Lithograph by F. M. Haskell & Company of Boston.*
RYSDYK'S HAMBLETONIAN: *In this lithograph by John J. Olone, after a painting by James H. Wright, we have the great Hambletonian with his owner William Rysdyk. Rysdyk paid $125 for the stallion, who was retired to stud at three and sired some 1,240 horses. Before he died in 1876, Hambletonian was getting a $500 stud fee for each live foal.*
VOLUNTEER: *Foaled in 1854, Volunteer was considered Hambletonian's most handsome son. Known first as Hambletonian, Jr., he was renamed during the Civil War. Mayer & Merkel of New York were the publishers.*

HARTFORD RACES

CHARTER OAK PARK

A GOOD RACE, WELL WON.

AUGUST 27, 28, 29, 30, 1889

PREMIUMS $36,000.00

INCLUDING THE

$10,000.00 STAKE

FOR THE

WINNERS OF THE GRAND CIRCUS.

T. O. KING, Secretary.

CURRIER & IVES ILLUMINATED RACE POSTERS, 115 NASSAU STREET, NEW YORK.

COL

SA

COLUMBUS, WINNER OF T

No. 1. Centreville, May 9th, 1830. Purse $300; 3 mile heats, under saddle, distanced Spot. Time 8m. 27½s.   2. Hunting Park, May 30th, 1830.
heats, under saddle, beat Cato, Tyro and Sweetbriar. Time 8m. 3½s. 8m. 16s. 8m. 15s.   4. Centreville, October 8th, 1832. Purse $200; 3 mile heats,
and Comet. Time 5m. 22s. 5m. 21s.   6. Harlæm, June 13th, 1833. Purse $200; heats thrice round, beat Collector and distanced Charley. Time 7m.
8m. 14s.   8. Centreville, December 2d, 1833. Match, stakes $300, heats best 3 in 5, under saddle, beat Comet in 3 heats. Time —. —.   9. Hu
heats, under saddle, beat Charlotte Temple. Time 8m. 2s. 8m. 5s.   11. Hunting Park, May, 1834. Purse $300; 3 mile heats, under saddle, beat Lady
ple. Time 7m. 4½s. 7m. 42s. 7m. 49s.   13. Centreville, October 3d, 1834. Purse $300; 3 mile heats, under saddle, beat Rolla. Time 8m. 5s. 8m. 6
1834. Purse $—; 3 mile heats, under saddle, beat Dread, Jackson and Spot. Time —. —.   16. Hunting Park, November 22d, 1834. Purse $200;
Centreville, October 1st, 1835. Purse $300; 3 mile heats, in harness, beat Rolla and Calvin Edson. Time 8m. 24½s. 8m. 20½s.   19. Trenton, April, 183
ness, beat Rolla and Fanny Pullen. Time 8m. 15s. 8m. 24s.   21. Beacon Course, May 10th, 1838. Purse $200; 2 mile heats, under saddle, beat Daniel We

RODE BY I

MBUS

ER.

Y-TWO MATCHES AND PURSES.

8 mile heats, under saddle, beat Ephraim Smooth, Top Gallant and Lady Jackson. Time 8m. 19s. 8m. 27s.   3. Centreville, May 6th, 1631. Purse $300 ; 3 mile
stanced Betsy Baker, Jerry and Crazy Jane Time 8m. 7s.   5. Hunting Park, October 18th, 1832. Purse $200 ; 2 mile heats, under saddle, beat "SALLY MILLER"
Course 109 yards, short of a mile.   7. Centreville, September 25th, 1833. Purse $300 ; 3 mile heats, under saddle, distanced Screw-driver and Collector. Time
ary 1st, 1834. Match, stakes $500, mile heats under saddle, beat Charlotte Temple in 2 heats. Time ——, ——.   10. Centreville, May 2d, 1834. Purse $300 ; 3 mile
rew-driver. Time 8m 7s. 8m. 11s.   12. Harlem, June 25th, 1834. Purse $200 ; heats thrice round the Course, under saddle, beat Confidence and Charlotte Tem-
unting Park, October, 1834. Purse $300 ; 3 mile heats, under saddle, beat Lady Jackson and Screw-driver in 2 heats. Time 7m. 57s. 8m. 3s.   15. Baltimore, ——
ur saddle, beat Dread. Time 5m. 28s. 5m. 47s.   17. Centreville, May 5th, 1835. Purse $300 ; 3 mile heats, under saddle, beat Rolla. Time 8m. 24s.   18.
, 3 mile heats, under saddle, beat Top Gallant, Comet and Lady Jackson, in 2 heats. Time ——, ——.   20. Centreville, May 17th, 1836. Purse $300 ; 3 mile heats, in har-
, 41s. 5m. 52.   22. Beacon Course, May 11th, 1833. Purse $200 ; mile heats best 3 in 5, under saddle, beat "Rattler." Time 2m. 47s. 2m. 46s. 2m. 47s. 2m. 48s.
R WHEALAY.

Entered according to Act of Congress in the Year

BELMONT PARK, PHILADELPHIA, PA.
TIME 2:17.
ROCHESTER, AUG. 10TH 1878.
TIME 2:15¾.

SMU

By Blanco, by Irons Cadm

WINNER OF

Sc

TIME, 2

OWNED BY HENRY

61 HANOVER ST. BOSTON, MASS

LER.

mus, by American Eclipse

ION PURSE

74

23 2:20.

LL, MILTON, MASS.

CLEVELAND DRIVING PARK JULY 27TH 1876.

TIME 2:16¼.

HARTFORD, CONN. AUG. 31ST 1876.

TIME 2:15¼.

Judge Fullerton

BEST TIME ON RECORD

Goldsmith Maid and Judge Fullerton, in the

Purse, $ 5,000 $ 2,500 to first, $ 1,500 to second, and $ 1,000 to the horse which beats 2:16

Goldsmith Maid

THREE HEATS IN 2:19¼. 2:16½ 2:16.

reat trot at east saginaw, mich. July 16ᵗʰ 1874.

udd Doble's b.m. Goldsmith Maid 1.1.1. B. Mace's ch.g. Judge Fullerton 2.2.2.

1. FANNY ALLEN. 2. BAY MARY. 3. IRONSIDES AND MATE. 4. HARRY O. 5. BLACK MAGGIE.   6. LADY LIGHTFOOT. 7. SUNBEAM. 8. YOUNG

TROTTING CRACKS OF PHILADELPHIA RETU

HAVING A BRUSH PAST TURNER'S HOTE

Respecfully Dedicated to the Lovers of Horses

TOR PATCHEN. 10. BAY GEORGE.   11. MACK. 12. RED CLOUD. 13. VICTORIA. 14. SUN-FLOWER. 15. GENERAL BIRNEY AND MATE.   16. MOSCOW. 17. JOE PARKER PONY, 18. NAPOLEON.

NG FROM THE RACE AT POINT BREEZE PARK,

PE FERRY ROAD, PHILADELPHIA, 1870.

Sporting Public in general by the Publisher.

PUBLISHED BY HASKELL & ALLEN,

Lancet

FEARNAUGH

STALLIONS,

LEAVING BRIGHTON HOTEL

OR THE MILL-DAM

PUBLISHED BY F. M. HASKELL & CO.,

RARUS,

Then, cocking the derby slightly to the left on his head, and drawing himself up to his full five feet seven and a half inches, he strode off through the open country toward Guerneville, a hard six hours' hike eastward; there a man could hire a ride toward San Francisco, seventy-five miles away.

By the time our gentleman bandit reached the big city, a report of his crime was on the desk of James B. Hume, head of the Wells Fargo police. And among the most important evidence was the message on the waybill. Jim Hume, a level-eyed, poker-faced man who had once ridden shotgun on stages himself, looked carefully at the four lines of the highwayman's message. They constituted, if you please, a poem, or anyway a verse:

> I've labored long and hard for bread
> for honor and for riches
> But on my corns too long you've tred,
> You fine haired Sons of Bitches.

This poetical work was not titled but it was signed, complete with a clue in the form of a kind of rebus in case anyone didn't recognize a poet when he read one: "BLACK BART, the Po8."

Jim Hume had never seen the name before, but the holdup man's method of operation was familiar. A hunt for just such a criminal had already been quietly under way for two years. It would last for six more. Over those eight years Black Bart, who was neither Bart nor black (he had lifted the name from a magazine story) racked up the amazing score of twenty-seven successful stage robberies out of twenty-eight tries—better than anyone before or since. He was always alone and on foot, never resorted to violence, and worked as methodically as a bookkeeper. He came to be old California's most famous road agent in spite of the fact that he went into the business when the lush days of the mining camps and $100,000 shipments of bullion were only golden memories. Old Bart's juiciest haul came to less than $5,000, and he didn't get to keep that one, for it was his last, and the one that finally tripped him. The sad fact is, gentlemanly Black Bart never did make a handsome living at his risky occupation. But he did manage to make a bit of history, and he has not been entirely forgotten: today in Mendocino County, California, one of the areas where he robbed stages, there is an annual carnival-like celebration known as Black Bart Days.

The "Po8" had waited until he was forty-five years old before deciding to collect by force what he felt the world owed him. Before that, he was plain Charley Boles, an easterner born in Jefferson County, New York, who had originally hustled out to California

Black Bart, one of the Old West's most successful road agents, dressed like a businessman, never fired his gun, and thoughtfully left little poems behind so the law would have no doubt who had pulled the job.

with the Gold Rush in 1850. He was twenty then, and though he hadn't found much gold by the time he drifted back eastward four years later, he had learned his way around parts of some mountainous northern California counties—Butte, Shasta, Trinity, El Dorado. He had an excellent sense of direction—and a long, long memory for topographical detail.

He never did get back to New York State. Illinois attracted him, and he bought a farm near Decatur. By the time the Civil War came he was married and had three little daughters, but he joined the 116th Illinois Infantry Volunteers nonetheless and served three years as a sergeant. (A decade or so later, like many another veteran of that war, he promoted himself—to captain.)

At war's end he was thirty-five, had sustained some minor wounds, and had no desire to return to the farm. He sold it, moved his family to Oregon, Illinois, and then decided to go to Montana. He went alone, and it was the last his dear Mary and the children ever saw of him. He did send them money for about two years, but then he stopped writing, and Mary became convinced that Indians had massacred him. (Much later, after his career as a road agent had ended and he was doing time, he wrote to her again, for a while. His letters were loving, but vague about plans to return home. He was a born drifter, and by then he seemed to know it.)

In 1875 he found himself in San Francisco. He may have come in that direction because he had a sister living in the vicinity. At any rate, 1875 was the critical year for Charley Boles. So far as we know, he had never stolen so much as a penny pencil, but now something pushed him a little too far. Perhaps he suddenly saw himself for what he was, a graying, middle-aged failure. He was bitter, or told himself he was, at the vested interests, and he seized upon the notion of squaring accounts by robbing some Wells Fargo stages. But he would be scrupulous about it, he promised himself: no robbing of passengers, no bloodshed; all he wanted was what the entrenched, moneyed interests had kept him from getting legitimately all his life.

His first stage robbery was in mountainous Calaveras County, east-northeast of San Francisco, the very county that Mark Twain's jumping-frog story made famous. He had decided on robbing the Sonora-to-Milton stage, and he'd picked a curve in the road flanked with big rocks. Shortly his technique was going to change in some respects, but on this first plunge he seems to have felt nervous about working without help, and he supplied the need in a way schoolboys know by heart: he cut six or eight gun-barrel-sized tree branches and wedged them between roadside rocks, pointing toward the place the stage would stop. And it actually worked, even though the driver was a veteran in the service.

"No use trying to do anything," he advised his passengers. "Look at those guns."

Down came the express box, and Boles chopped it open. What it yielded, Wells Fargo did not reveal—they were often close-mouthed about losses, not caring to entice incipient thieves with too many luscious facts—but it was enough to encourage Boles in his new career. This was July; he lay low for five whole months and then planned another job three days after Christmas, shifting to the countryside about fifty miles north of Sacramento.

Again he got enough to make it interesting, and after another five-month layoff he pulled his third job, also in northern California. After his first holdup he dropped the tree-branch guns, maybe because he had not removed them and the ruse had been discovered on the stage's return trip. But the flour-sack mask and the duster were enough to stamp all the holdups as the work of one man, and so was his invariable four-word command to the stage driver: "Throw down the box."

Until he gave himself a name, he was anonymous. Then, on his fourth holdup—he had let fourteen months pass this time between jobs—he gave the lawmen a handle to use, and he was from then on Black Bart the Po8.

No poet—or Po8—ever rode to fame on so meager an output. In his whole career Bart wrote but two poems, though he did claim to have had a third ready for job No. 29, the one he never got to pull. The second, and last, poem was again written on a waybill and was left at the scene of his fifth stage robbery. It consisted of two new stanzas with the first poem sandwiched between. The two new stanzas read:

> here I lay me down to Sleep
> to wait the coming Morrow
> perhaps Success perhaps defeat
> And everlasting Sorrow
>
> let come what will 'Ill try it on
> My condition can't be worse
> And if theres money in that Box
> Tis Munny in my purse

He purposely vulgarized the spelling and punctuation for he knew better, as his letters home show very clearly.

This fifth stage robbery, on July 25, 1878, almost a year after the fourth one, was in the mountainous Feather River country of north-central California. While still no bonanza, it did bring Bart about $600 in coin and equivalents.

BEADLE'S

Dime New York Library

COPYRIGHTED IN 1884, BY BEADLE & ADAMS.

ENTERED AT THE POST OFFICE AT NEW YORK, N. Y., AT SECOND CLASS MAIL RATES.

Vol. XXII.   Published Every Wednesday.   *Beadle & Adams, Publishers,*   98 WILLIAM STREET, N. Y., February 27, 1884.   Ten Cents a Copy. $5.00 a Year   No. 279

THE GOLD-DRAGON; or, THE CALIFORNIA-BLOODHOUND.

A STORY OF Po-8, THE LONE HIGHWAYMAN.

BY WILLIAM H. MANNING.

In February of 1884, only three months after Black Bart's capture, Beadle & Adams of New York had this dime novel on the stands, its Dickensian plot based loosely—very loosely —on the Po8's career. In the fictitious episode illustrated on its cover, a villain named Surly Steve Storms tries to steal the hooded highwayman's loot; as they grapple near a stream, Detective Ned Neverfail swims quietly alongside, hides the loot underwater, and later brings Bart to book. Steve drowns. Bart goes to jail. Ned (naturally) wins The Girl.

By this time, Bart had settled into a pattern for his robberies in every respect except the time lapse between them, which was erratic. That may have been dictated simply by economic need, for Bart was not greedy. The most amazing thing is that this quite conservative man should have become so successful a thief. Or perhaps his conservatism *was* the explanation: his cautious methods made him very difficult to catch.

Wells Fargo's Detective Hume knew that he couldn't expect a great deal of help from sheriffs in the counties where stage robberies occurred: few of them were really good at careful police work. Hume, a big, quiet man who usually had a cigar clamped between his teeth, was on his own. But in the duel of wits with Black Bart, Hume held the best cards, and in the end the winning ones: experience, the better mind, the organization to back him. Another trump was added after Bart's fifth holdup—a reward. The governor of California, William Irwin, offered $300 for Bart's capture; Wells Fargo matched it; the post office department—whose pouches Bart regularly slit open and plundered, ignoring the fact that the mail was not necessarily owned by the vested interests he was supposed to be fighting—added $200 more. To collect this total of $800, a person would have to capture Black Bart and produce the evidence needed to land him in jail. But for the one who succeeded there was the possibility of added compensation, for it was customary to give a road agent's captor one-quarter of any booty that might be recovered.

For a while at least, instead of helping bring him to book, Black Bart's victims exalted him into an awesome legend, a superman who appeared out of nowhere and vanished into nothingness. It was so unusual for a highwayman to walk any distance, let alone across rugged open country, that it is no wonder the legend was embroidered with tales of a phantom horse, or of a devil's disciple flying by dark of night.

So it was that as he continued his road-agentry, the man who had been a failure all his life found himself an immense success. Although he relished it hugely, he hardly ever talked about it to anyone. But one day in the fall of 1880, about ten days after his thirteenth stage robbery, Bart was in Sonoma County, about 150 miles south of where the holdup had taken place. On foot as usual and finding himself still a distance from food and lodging at sundown, he took potluck with a lone logger, one Elisha Shortridge, who had a ranch west of Santa Rosa.

By this time Bart had abandoned the use of the cumbersome valise. Law officers found it beside a creek but could extract no useful clues from it (fingerprints as a police tool did not come into use until after the nineteenth century had ended). When he met the logger, Bart was carrying a bedroll over his shoulder and was cradling his shotgun, so that Shortridge took him for a hunter. Afterward the logger said, "Just two things about him struck me. His voice sounded like he was talking into an empty barrel, and he had eyes that seemed to look clear through you." He added: "I thought maybe he was looking the country over, sizing up land and timber."

Bart corrected that error the next morning. After breakfast, Shortridge was giving the stranger's gun a friendly once-over, a usual thing between gun fanciers, and noticed that it was an early type of breech-loader.

CONTINUED ON PAGE 89

53

A WHISTLE GOOD-BYE

Text and photographs by DAVID PLOWDEN

An era is ending on America's inland waterways. A century and a half after it began—with the launching of Robert Fulton's *North River Steamboat* in 1807—the Age of Steam is chuffing to a close. At its height there were overnight and day-excursion steamers; packets carrying passengers, mail, and goods on regularly scheduled runs; ferries taking people to and from work; vessels for carrying cargo, pushing barges, or clearing channels. Powered by reciprocating steam engines and driven at first by paddle wheels and later by propellers, they plied our coasts, crisscrossed our lakes and harbors, and along our navigable rivers caused whole towns to spring up. Almost all these steamboats are gone now. Bulk-cargo carriers, a few railroad-car ferries, and one overnight steamer still ply the Great Lakes; some ferries, workboats, and excursion boats are still to be seen on the Mississippi and a few other rivers. But the coastal steamers are virtually extinct, and on Long Island Sound—in bygone days the greatest steamboat showcase in North America—there is only a single survivor, the ferryboat *Catskill*. Two excursion steamboats operate out of New York Harbor, but a quarter of a century ago there were forty-five. Canada has taken its overnight luxury liners off the Great Lakes and the St. Lawrence. Waterway traffic is far from dead: it has made a spectacular comeback since World War II and last year carried a healthy ten per cent of the nation's freight. But today's businesslike, diesel-driven towboats and gasoline-engine barges are a far cry from the graceful steamboats of the past, with their churning paddle wheels, lordly pilothouses, and slender stacks. I took most of these pictures within the last five years, yet so fast does Progress bear down upon us that what began as a personal salute has ended as a farewell to steam.

The feathered stacks and ornate pilothouse of a New Orleans ferry recall the great days of Mississippi steamboating. The Edwin N. Bisso's *future, like that of most surviving river and lake steamers, is uncertain.*

54

EDWIN N. BISSO.

The yeomen of the inland waterways are the workboats, which spend their lives doing essential chores without fanfare. They will not be doing them much longer by steam. The catamaran ferry *City of Baton Rouge* (right) and her sister ship *Louisiana* will soon be replaced by a new bridge over the Mississippi between Baton Rouge and Port Allen. The propeller-driven dredger *Ockerson* (opposite page, top) will soon be retired by the Corps of Engineers, which has already retired the *Arkansas II* (below), a snag boat that once cleared obstructions and set out navigation buoys on the Mississippi. The two New York Central tugboats opposite, part of the last sizable steam-tug fleet in North America, will probably puff their last when the Central-Pennsylvania merger allows the Pennsy's new diesels to take over in New York Harbor. Next to them is the laker *Diamond Alkali*. She and her fellow cargo carriers *William J. Filbert* and *Algosoo* (whose graceful stern is seen just beneath the *Alkali*) carry ore and grain from the top of Lake Superior to Chicago, Detroit, and the Lake Erie ports via the Soo Canal locks; they return with steel and coal. They are fighting a determined rear-guard action against the new breed of diesel giants fostered by the St. Lawrence Seaway. The wooden-hulled, coal-fired, twin-stacked *Lone Star* (below center) noses barges up and down the Mississippi River near Davenport, Iowa. Fifty years ago she would have been commonplace, but now she is the sole surviving classic Mississippi steamboat. Mark Twain would have loved her.

The Yeomen of the Waterways

OVERLEAF: *The railroad-car ferry Lansdowne, loaded with truck trailers and boxcars full of auto frames, slips through the mists of the Detroit River on her way to Windsor, Ontario. Built in 1884, she is the continent's oldest working paddle boat.*

steamers left. The Peter Stuyvesant *is afloat but inactive. The* Hamilton's *stacks still bear the emblem of the Day Line, dead since 1948.*

The Mississippi and the Hudson each developed a distinctive style of passenger steamboat. Today the original Mississippi boats have all but vanished, but the Hudson retains the classic *Alexander Hamilton* (above). On the Mississippi system there are two steamboats, the *Belle of Louisville* and the *Delta Queen*, both stern-wheelers, but the *Queen* was built for service on the Sacramento River in California, and the *Belle* was a ferry. Now the *Queen* is the only passenger vessel on which one can travel extensively on our inland rivers; her cruises have been so successful that her owners, Greene Line Steamers of Cincinnati, plan to build a new steel steam packet in nineteenth-century style. And the *Belle of Louisville,* with her pilothouse relocated amidships, her stacks lengthened, and a Texas deck added, bears some resemblance to the great floating palaces of the past.

Mr. Plowden is a New York free-lance photographer with a fine eye for vanishing Americana. This article is adapted from his new book, Farewell to Steam, *just published by the Stephen Greene Press. The farewell is to locomotives as well as steamboats.*

The race over, a band salutes the winning Queen. *She cruises regularly on the Ohio, Kentucky, Tennessee, and Mississippi.*

COLLECTION OF PAUL H. BONNER, JR.

Aces, with
kibitzing kings,
queens, and a few
other cards

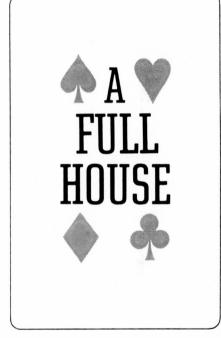

How many can you remember?
For identification, and
a reminiscence by a member
of the next generation,
turn the page

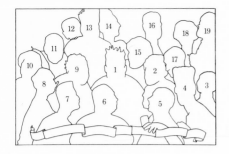

♠♥ A FULL HOUSE ♦♣

By HEYWOOD HALE BROUN

The origins of the Thanatopsis Plea-
sure and Inside Straight Club lie
somewhere between a bar in Paris and
the apartment of Harold Ross, its dis-
solution somewhere between a room
above the Colony Restaurant and the
Long Island home of Herbert Bayard
Swope.

At its zenith it occupied quarters in
the Algonquin Hotel and the Saturday
nights of as colorful a group of poker
players as ever sat down together outside a Bret Harte short story. It was
sometimes called the Thanatopsis *Literary* and Inside Straight Club, and the
honor of founding it was, at different
times, claimed by or for F. P. Adams,
Alexander Woollcott, Ross, and a press
agent named John Peter Toohey.

The Thanatopsis was a part of New
York in the twenties, a city and a time
that seem as far away and wonderful
to us now as Athens and the Age of
Pericles appeared to the lonely literates
of the early Middle Ages. New York
was then a city of infinite promise to
the talented. Loose inside its skin like
a healthy puppy, the town had lots of
room for the dreamers who poured into
it after World War I, ready to set the
place on its ear with plays, poems,
novels, paintings, sculpture, music, acting and all the other ways of shooting
a rocket at the bright star of fame. In
those days there were plenty of lofts for
artists, garrets for poets, walk-ups for
playwrights and actors; and at lunch-
time there was the Round Table in the
Rose Room of the Algonquin.

New York is an old dog now, with
smoke-dimmed eyes and office buildings for fleas. The artists and writers
are thinly scattered across its boroughs
and suburbs, and no single group
wields the critical power or sets the
cultural tone of the city as did the circle that lunched at the Round Table
and, with some changes of cast, played
poker at the Thanatopsis Club.

"The first game was played," wrote
Frank Adams years afterward, "at the
apartment then jointly occupied by two
recently returned members of the 1918
Stars and Stripes staff, Pvt. Harold W.

Ross and Pvt. John T. Winterich. Sgt.
Alexander Woollcott, Heywood Broun
and I were at that first game."

The name was stolen from Sinclair
Lewis' *Main Street:* "And of course
there's our women's study club—the
Thanatopsis Club . . . they've made
the city plant ever so many trees, and
they run the rest room for farmers'
wives. And they do take such an interest in refinement and culture. So—in
fact, so very unique."

After meeting for a while in various
other apartments, the club settled into
the Algonquin, whose owner, Frank
Case, had offered them the use of a
room. The Thanatopsians stayed there
for a number of years, usually starting
right after the Round Table broke up
its Saturday luncheon and continuing,
on occasion, straight through to Monday morning. Along the way there
would be cases of what Adams called
"Winners' Sleeping Sickness" and
"Losers' Insomnia, or Broun's Disease,"
but new players were recruited from
the ring of kibitzers which always surrounded the table. Some of these were
subs waiting the call from the bench;
some were friends or wives of the con-
testants; many were wide-eyed newcomers from Colorado or Kansas. These
younger people were much awed by
the Presences and remained alertly at-
tentive to the possibility of profound,
or at least witty, remarks.

Much of what they heard sounded
like the dialogue at a game in the cellar of a fraternity house. When, for
instance, Raoul Fleischmann drew the
perfect poker hand, there was a good
deal of merriment over calling him
Royal Flushman all evening.

My father, given some indifferent
wine on a rainy night, remarked, "Oh
well, any port in a storm," a remark
so well received that he looked forward
to bad weather and wine so that he
might repeat the performance.

Although the two lowest cards in the
deck get you off to a bad start in a stud
game, George Kaufman would always
take them so he could remark as he
folded that he had been "trey-deuced."

A frequent kibitzer at these games was a wide-eyed, sweet-faced, priggish little boy, myself, whose principal function was to act as straight man in a small vaudeville routine of my father's. It would begin by his remarking to me as I wandered around the table that he had recently been to the zoo. Obediently I would ask if he had seen any beasts that particularly interested him. Yes, he would reply, there had been a pair of fascinating oxlike animals, and when he stood between their cages he had been reminded of a cigar. Prompted by a piping "Which cigar?" he would say, "Between the Yaks."

There were group rituals, such as intoning "As the girl said to the sailor" in chorus after some remark deemed appropriate to the tag, which was left over from an A.E.F. story not suitable for reprinting in whole or part; rising and singing "He remains a god-damn fool," to the tune of Gilbert and Sullivan's "He Remains an Englishman," after bad poker plays; addressing Toohey as Our Founder, after which Toohey always rose and bowed; and a whole clutch of other cries, songs, and clubby "inside" things.

The usual pattern of the game itself was three rounds of draw followed by a round of stud, no wild cards and no seven-card games. It was, in fact, very much like a game on Main Street, except that one cannot imagine Harpo Marx in Gopher Prairie, and there were more ladies on the edge of the game, or in it, than there were likely to have been in Minnesota.

The country-born club members weren't too happy about women in the game, but Viola Toohey was accounted a good player, as was Margaret Swope. Ross's wife, Jane Grant, occasionally took a hand to hold the franchise for woman's rights. My mother, Ruth Hale, another feminist leader, claimed she could play as well as the men if she wanted to play a game as dull as poker.

Helen Hayes, Ina Claire, Lynn Fontanne, Margalo Gillmore, and other great ladies of the theater watched almost every Saturday night after their performances, but the only G. L. of the T. who ever played was Alice Brady, who had the whole club to her apartment and by cheerfully inept play lost a great deal of money, distressing the

more gallant of her guests. The worriers were later cheered to discover that Miss Brady had just signed a Hollywood contract for more money than was earned by a whole table of editors, writers, and press agents.

Dorothy Parker was often present, never played, said little, and missed nothing.

It's perhaps a little unfair to leave the impression that nothing but cracker-barrel japery was ever heard around the poker board. After all, with so many black-belt wits in the game, so many who could splinter a plank with the edge of a phrase, there were bound to be some wonderful falls taken at one time or another. It is simply that the general feeling was one of unbuttoned relaxation, very different from the Mermaid Tavern competitions of the Round Table downstairs. The Thanatopsis Club was perhaps the one place where all the erstwhile small-town boys who had to slick their hair down and talk fancy most of the time could get off the treadmill of sophistication for a few hours.

A question asked every Saturday night was "What are we playing for?" Almost every night the announced stakes were a little steeper as the country moved into the great boom, as the talents of the players began to be more richly rewarded in the outside world, as some of the already well-to-do players like Swope, Fleischmann, and Gerald Brooks wanted more action.

Our house on Eighty-fifth Street became ours because my father had a good streak at the Thanatopsis in 1921, picking up $1,000 over the course of several sessions. For this sum and his signature on four, count 'em, four mortgages, we were able to move into the house. If any fact were needed to show you the faraway and long-ago quality of New York in those days, it is that such a sum could make you the proprietor of a four-story brownstone.

Boom psychology was everywhere, as the twenties roared to a close, and the Thanatopsis said good-bye to the Algonquin—where they used to bypass room service and bring in bags of delicatessen—and moved to a room above the Colony Restaurant, where a touch of a button brought a soft-footed servitor with a menu and a wine list.

The soft-footed servitors didn't hear much laughter, however, as the game kept getting bigger, and relaxation was chased up the wall by anxiety.

In F.P.A.'s *Diary of Our Own Samuel Pepys,* a loose chronicle of the doings of himself and his cronies, there are mentions of "tiny meetings" of the club and occasional weekday meetings when it appeared that Saturday was too full of other things to do. Once near the turn of the magic decade he wonders, "Whatever happened to the silly old Thanatopsis?" It is mentioned again after that, and it probably held a last meeting sometime in 1931, by which time most of the really big poker players had moved on to Swope's house in Sands Point, which could hold a clutch of Thanatopsians and a gaggle of society folk anxious to meet the fur-trimmed Bohemians whose jokes they read in the columns, whose plays they saw, whose books they read, whose somehow special lives they envied.

The world had long been an oyster for the club members, and now in the high noon of their careers they began to gather the pearls. Royalties, salaries, and fees were up along with the market, and out to Long Island the talented parvenus went to meet Society on the croquet lawn, over the backgammon board, and at the poker table. They didn't need support from each other any more, and their ways began to diverge as they went out into a world that still didn't quite believe there was going to be a depression. By the time everyone believed it, the different ways had become very different indeed, and nostalgia holds a hammer lock on many of them yet.

Still, they had been like their Gopher Prairie sisters, "So—in fact, so very unique," and unlike the G.P. ladies, busy with their trees and rest rooms, they had filled—at the poker table and away from it—an awful lot of inside straights.

In 1949 Mr. Broun, after several years as a columnist and sports writer, became an actor—on Broadway and off, on the straw-hat circuit, and in TV and radio. In 1940 he edited a collection of his father's columns, and last year he wrote a book on the theatre entitled A Studied Madness.

Hush-a-bye, Indiana

By WILLIAM E. WILSON

During my undergraduate years at Harvard College, the Commonwealth of Massachusetts was preparing for an official celebration of the three-hundredth anniversary of the royal charter that created the Massachusetts Bay Colony. One of my favorite professors in those days was Charles Townsend Copeland, known affectionately among his students as "Copey," a man to whom legends clung like steel filings on a magnet; and one of my favorites among those legends—whether true or apocryphal I cannot say—was the story of Copey and the Massachusetts Tercentenary Committee for Monuments and Memorials. When asked by the committee to suggest appropriate sites for historical markers, Copey, so the story ran, proposed a tablet in the heart of Cambridge

Common bearing an inscription that read: *On this spot on April 1, 1630, Prudence Goodchild was raped by a friendly Indian.*

Most of us laughed at Copey's little joke for the wrong reasons. The predicament of a Puritan maiden encountering an oversociable redskin within our academic purlieus was too beguiling an image for us to realize that Copey had something else in mind, to recognize that he was holding up to sly ridicule the rape of history itself by local pride and press agentry. Now, many years later, confronted as I am at this writing by a sesquicentennial celebration in my native state of Indiana, I find my old professor's April-Fool's-Day joke often coming to mind. Once more Prudence Goodchild is in for a fate worse than death, for Hoosiers are not only a prideful breed; they are also, like Prudence's Indian, famous for their sociability.

It does not require an official celebration to bring out these characteristics and to give local mythmakers self-justification for the ravishing of truth. I grew up in southern Indiana, where my father used to say the fence rails he had seen in his lifetime that were attributed to Abe Lincoln's axe and maul were enough to make all creation bull-safe and hog-tight. At the same time, he contended—and rightly, too, as I later discovered in research and conversations in that region while writing a book about Lincoln—if every ancestor so claimed had indeed been Abe's "constant companion" in his youth, Abe would have been at all times so crowded by a press of cronies in his Spencer County days that he would never have had room to swing an axe. Apparently the first principle of excessive enthusiasm for a region's past is to assert significant relationships with history—whether they exist or not.

Another principle on which such pride operates at the risk of Prudence's chastity is the recognition of only those facts that will be popularly and comfortably received in one's neighborhood, cherishing and perpetuating ignorance of anything that might be unpopular and uncomfortable. This grim determination on the part of local historians was demonstrated to me often while I was writing a Rivers of America volume about the Wabash country, and most notably perhaps in relation to my pursuit of information about Theodore Dreiser, Indiana's extra-territorially most renowned and intramurally least admired of literary figures.

In the 1880's, ten-year-old Theodore Dreiser and his mother were brought to Evansville, Indiana, and established in a brick cottage on East Franklin Street by Theodore's older brother, Paul, who had changed his name to Dresser and who himself lived at that time with a mistress, Sallie Walker, alias Annie Brace, madam of the most sumptuous house of prostitution on the city's waterfront. When I visited the Franklin Street cottage in 1939, there was a large sign on the front lawn that read: *Home of Paul Dresser, Composer of "On the Banks of the Wabash."* I could not restrain myself from telling the woman who showed me through the cottage that Paul Dresser had not lived in it but his more famous brother, Theodore Dreiser, had. "Who," she asked me, suspiciously, "is Theodore Dreiser?" Obviously she did not know; but even after I told her, she preferred the myth about the sentimental songwriter to the truth about the naturalistic

novelist, for the sign remained as it was for several years thereafter. (Today that sign is gone, but now there is a sign over the door of the cottage, and it reads, *The Dresser*. As for the fancy house on the waterfront, it continued to flourish until a few years ago, but to my knowledge it never bore a marker of any kind to advertise the apartment that was once shared by the beloved Hoosier vaudeville singer and the madam of the place.)

At the end of a chapter on Indiana authors in *The Wabash*, I gave Theodore Dreiser credit for writing the words of the famous nostalgic song composed by his brother, basing my statement on a passage from Dreiser's own portrait of Dresser, "My Brother Paul," in the volume entitled *Twelve Men*. In that essay Dreiser said, "I took a piece of paper and after meditating a while scribbled in the most tentative manner imaginable the first verse and chorus of that song almost as it was published."

This revelation inspired a rain of letters and telegrams from irate Hoosiers as soon as the book was published. "If Dreiser wrote the verses of that song," one Indianian protested, "Hoosiers will have to learn their history all over again and Terre Haute will have to rename its bridge." The Indianapolis *Star* ran an editorial denouncing me for my calumny and referring to me toploftily as "a downstate schoolmaster," although at that time I dwelt in Rhode Island, had not lived in Indiana for twelve years, and had never presided over a Hoosier schoolroom. The Chicago *Tribune* published a story about the controversy, pointing out that even in Illinois people knew that Dreiser did not write "On the Banks of the Wabash." And annually thereafter, for more than a decade, I received indignant letters from a local historian of Terre Haute who always concluded, "Yours maybe."

69

ILLUSTRATED FOR AMERICAN HERITAGE BY MICHAEL RAMUS

I half-expected the protests I received from residents of Indiana, but I did not expect the response that came from Theodore Dreiser himself. Dreiser wrote to Lewis Gannett, who published the letter in his column in the New York *Herald Tribune*:

"It troubles me no little that William E. Wilson should have credited me with the authorship of 'On the Banks of the Wabash.' If I had written 'My Brother Paul' after I achieved an international literary reputation I certainly would never have as much as mentioned the fact that I had contributed one word—for, knowing the weight of influence that goes with a wide reputation as I came to know it later, I would then have understood how a part of the public, at least, might have swung to the belief that I had written it of course. There was no lie told, but had I realized for an instant that with some my statement might have taken a little of the glitter from my brother I certainly would not have written what I did."

Years later, I learned from W. A. Swanberg's biography of Dreiser that the Hoosier novelist composed this equivocal message while he was in California "trying to sell to the films the story based on Paul's career, called *My Gal Sal,* making use of 'On the Banks of the Wabash' and others of his songs."

Another product of local pride is the deliberate changing of history to suit the historian's convenience, especially if such changes make history more dramatic. No less a man than Theodore Roosevelt fell into this habit from time to time: witness his imaginative ac-

count of George Rogers Clark's capture of Kaskaskia in *The Winning of the West.* Roosevelt, I suspect, was the model for a Hoosier Herodotus of the 1920's and 1930's who, posing as a professor at Indiana University, which he never was, used to conduct "historical" tours of the state (for a financial consideration) and describe the dramas of the past in the neighborhoods where they occurred. This man was a master at wrong emphasis, legerdemain with facts, conscienceless scene-shifting, and spellbinding oratory. In New Harmony, scene of the Utopian experiments of German Harmonites and of Robert Owen's advocates of the New Moral World, the story is still told of one occasion when the tour conductor stood at the New Harmony ferry landing and described the arrival of the Owenites' Boatload of Knowledge. (Actually the boatload of philosophers and scientists was unloaded in 1826 several miles upstream from the ferry landing of a century later, but that point had become inaccessible in modern times and, anyhow, at the ferry landing there was a little park suitable for a gathering of tourists.) After the speaker finished his dramatic story, a native of the region who happened to be nearby stood up and said, "Mister, that's a goddam lie. In them days the Wabash didn't flow within three miles of here."

Most exasperating, if perhaps the least harmful, of all the wiles of Prudence Goodchild's Indian in any locality are the boosterism, sanctimony, and hokum that emphasize the inconsequential and trumpet the improbable. In the twelve-month which began in

Indiana on April 19, the date when President Madison in 1816 signed the Enabling Act that admitted our state to the Union, the Hoosier version of Uncle Sam is being resurrected, as is "the Betsy Ross of the Northwest," one Madame Godare of Vincennes, and we are being told again—and often (whether true or not, who cares?)—that the first night baseball game was played in Fort Wayne in 1883, that Anne Baxter, actress, Red Skelton, comedian, Norman Norell, fashion designer, and Dan Patch, racehorse, were born in Indiana.

Throughout this sesquicentennial year, many Hoosiers will continue to believe that the Old Oaken Bucket, for whose possession the football teams of Indiana and Purdue universities battle annually, is the "subject of the famous James Whitcomb Riley poem," to quote a Hoosier public-relations firm, although Samuel Woodworth of the *New York Mirror* wrote those verses thirty years before Riley was born. Memorial beards will continue to grow in profusion, although beards were not in fashion in 1816; attics will be rifled for anachronistic costumes to be worn in inaccurate local pageants; and the governor will dub a whole tribe of "Sagamores of the Wabash," honoring prominent residents of a state which, although named for Indians, was never thickly populated by them.

Indiana is not, of course, an isolated phenomenon in this respect. Such hubris as Copey held up to ridi-

cule with his story of Prudence Goodchild is manifest everywhere. I have lived in seven states of the Union and have endured a heptad—if I may extend the official idiom for such celebrations—of tercentenaries, bicentennials, centennials, and semicentennials, and a quindecad of lesser decennials and quinquennials, and I have witnessed the same rapacious prevarication and exaggeration in each of them. Everyone knows that if all the New Englanders who claim ancestors on the *Mayflower* were telling the truth, that tiny ship would have sunk at its moorings from overloading before it left Plymouth Harbor; that George Washington did not live enough nights to sleep in all those cherished beds up and down the Atlantic Coast; that Daniel Boone must have been permanently and ubiquitously "bewildered," if not indeed "lost," if he wandered over all the western territory claimed as his stamping ground; that Fort Knox itself could not contain the gold nuggets reputed to have come from Sutter's Mill; and that the Confederate colonels who populated the South for almost a century after the Irrepressible Conflict could have staffed the combined armies of the First and Second World Wars. Human nature being what it is, Prudence Goodchild's friendly Indian will probably never become a Vanishing American.

In addition to books on the Wabash, on Abraham Lincoln, and on New Harmony, Mr. Wilson has written Indiana: A History, *published by the Indiana University Press.*

interpreters, and guides; forty-five French-Canadian *engagés;* and an Indian woman and her two children. She was a stolid and uncomplaining Iowa known as Marie Aioe, the wife of Pierre Dorion, one of the expedition's interpreters.

The travellers crossed South Dakota, guided by Hoback, Reznor, and Robinson, as well as by Edward Rose, a man of dubious character who had also come up the Missouri with Lisa in 1807, and had subsequently lived with the Crow Indians on the plains. The Astorians met a band of Cheyennes, skirted the slopes of the Black Hills, and, entering northeastern Wyoming, travelled across the rough, rolling grassland and the ravines of the Powder River's tributaries toward the Big Horn Mountains. In the foothills of that range a band of Crows joined them, and Hunt was fearful at first that, perhaps assisted by Edward Rose, their former companion, those Indians would pillage the expedition. He and his men maintained their guard; and although Rose gave the others reason to believe he was plotting with the Crows against them, no conflict occurred. The Indians traded amicably, and then helped guide the party to a pass that led across the Big Horns. When the Crows rode away, Hunt offered Rose half a year's wages, three horses, traps, and "some other things" if he would quit the expedition and stay with the Crows. Accepting the offer, Rose hurried after the Indians, and Hunt was glad to be rid of him.

On the west side of the Big Horns, the expedition came on the Bighorn River, and on September 9 turned up the valley of its tributary, the Wind River, down which the three Kentuckians had come earlier in the year. Near present-day Dubois, Wyoming, the men began to suffer from a scarcity of game. Learning from an Indian of a pass that led southwestward across the Wind River Mountains to another river where buffalo were plentiful, Hunt abruptly turned the group in that direction, despite the lateness of the season for mountain travelling and the fact that he was leaving a direct, shorter route to his goal for a longer and more uncertain one. Climbing the Wind River Mountains to present-day Union Pass, the men beheld an inspiring view of the Teton range, still far distant in the west. The Kentuckians told them that those snow-capped peaks overlooked the head of the river on which they had wintered, and the Astorians named them the Pilot Knobs, sighting on them repeatedly for the direction toward which they would eventually have to turn.

Descending the mountains, they arrived at the headwaters of the Green River, which the trappers called the Spanish River because they believed that Spaniards

A St. Louis civic leader in his later years, Wilson Price Hunt looked like anything but a mountain man and fur trader.

lived along its banks somewhere to the south. The high valley, stirring with herds of buffalo, was beautiful, carpeted with grass and cut by sparkling streams that tumbled from the mountains. The area was a favorite summer hunting ground and rendezvous area for Shoshonis, and in one of the narrow side canyons the expedition came on a camp of Indians drying buffalo meat for the winter. Some of the natives had had previous contact with parties of Lisa's men, and they were pleased to trade meat and a few beaver skins with the newcomers. Hunt was quick to recognize the area as excellent beaver country. He urged the Shoshonis to continue to hunt beaver, and promised to send a party of his men to live among them and trade for the furs they gathered.

Leaving the Indians on September 24, the expedition moved northwestward over a rugged and difficult divide between the waters of the Green and the Snake and reached a stream which Hoback, one of the Kentuckians, recognized: he had trapped it the previous winter. Following that river, which is still known as the Hoback, the men arrived at the Snake near present-day Jackson, Wyoming, and realized that they would have been there much earlier if they had remained on the Kentuckians' route all the way up the Wind River valley and over the present Togwótee Pass to what is now called Jackson Hole.

The Snake, viewed as a headwater of the Columbia, was greeted with joy. Many of the men, notably Joseph Miller, one of the partners, had had their fill of horseback travel over the rugged, precipitous terrain, and they regarded the rest of the journey as a relatively easy one by water. Hunt spent several days, however, having his men search for trees large enough for the construction of dugout canoes. In the meantime, he sent out four men of the company with orders to stay in the Jackson Hole area and trap its streams. When

OVERLEAF: *The wintry terrain of southern Idaho rolls into the sunrise, looking much as it did to Hunt's party.*

they had collected a sufficient stock of furs, they were to make their way to the mouth of the Columbia or to any intermediate post that the company might build in the interior.

On October 1, Hunt's men were still trying to find timber suitable for canoes. That day Hunt wrote in his journal, "It rained in the valley and snowed in the mountains." Two days later it rained and sleeted all day. An unexpected crisis arose when an exploratory party under John Reed reported impassable rapids and narrow canyons on the river below them. Despite Miller's objection, Hunt now decided to abandon the plan to take to the river and, instead, to continue by horseback and hurry across the Teton Mountains ahead of him, which he believed were the last on their route. On October 5 the party left the river and, guided by the Kentuckians and two Shoshoni Indians, climbed the mountains and crossed the snow-whitened summit of Teton Pass into present-day Idaho. Three days later, hoping they had seen the last of the menacing snowy heights, the travellers rode through "a beautiful plain" and reached the deserted log huts in which the Kentuckians and their companions, under the leadership of Andrew Henry, had spent the previous winter. Nearby was the north fork of the Snake, known ever since as Henrys Fork, more peaceful and promising than the fork east of the mountains. Timber thick enough for canoes was also available, and Hunt set his men to work constructing craft for the descent of the river. Meanwhile, deciding to use the cabins for a company post, he retained the two Shoshonis to care for the expedition's horses and to watch over the huts until he could send a permanent party back to the area.

Hoback, Reznor, and Robinson, joined by another hunter, now detached themselves from the expedition, planning to trap streams with which they were familiar and to explore new ones. At the same time, Joseph Miller, apparently still smarting from Hunt's failure to take his advice on the eastern side of the Tetons, suddenly announced that he too would remain in this region and try his luck trapping with the Kentuckians. Hunt was crestfallen, but was unable to deter Miller, who was determined to go no farther with him.

The desertion cast a pall over the company, but on October 19 the travellers bade farewell to the five who would stay behind and, leaving the cabins, embarked in fifteen canoes on Henrys Fork, at that point a fast but placid stream. As it turned out, the decision to give up horses and to take to the river was a tragic mistake; but no white man had been on this stretch of the Snake River before, and none of the Astorians could foresee the perils that lay between them and the river's lower section, which they knew that Lewis and Clark had successfully navigated.

At first there was no sign of danger, and Hunt looked forward confidently to a short and swift journey. Then, as the men passed the junction of the two forks of the Snake and the main river broadened, they met rapids and falls that filled their canoes with water, carried off some of their possessions, and forced them to make difficult portages. On October 28, near present-day Burley in southern Idaho, they entered an awesome canyon and shot through a frightening stretch of roaring white water. One of the canoes smashed into a rock, and its French-Canadian steersman was toppled into the water and swept away. The accident brought the expedition to a sober halt. While most of the men waited with the canoes, Hunt and three members of the party climbed laboriously to the top of the basalt cliffs that hemmed the stream and walked thirty-five miles downriver, surveying what lay ahead of them. The river was unlike any they had ever seen or heard about before. It ran fast at the bottom of a deep gash in the level plain, boiling and tossing below barren and precipitous canyon walls that were so high and dangerous that there were only two places where Hunt could climb down to get water to drink. A reconnoitering group that explored along the opposite rim of the canyon came back with a more optimistic report; but four canoes that were portaged six miles down on that side of the river were immediately thereafter swept away with equipment and guns, and the men concluded that further travel by water was impossible.

The expedition was suddenly in a perilous position, without horses, running out of food, and isolated in the vast, unexplored Snake plains, apparently empty of game and as bleak and arid as a desert. In a hurried attempt to solve the problem, Hunt impulsively split up his party and sent out four small groups. One, under Ramsay Crooks, was to walk all the way back to Henry's cabins, which they estimated to be about 340 miles behind them, and return with their horses. Two other groups, under Reed and McClellan, were to continue downriver on foot and search for Indians who could provide them with food. The fourth, under Donald McKenzie, was to strike north across the desolate plain and try to find the Columbia River. The fragmentation of the party seemed the only hope, but

CONTINUED ON PAGE 91

In a bleak country of high hills, to which they retreated south out of Hell's Canyon, Hunt's party came on Shoshoni Indian horses, like those seen at right nuzzling through the powdery snow for grass. The hungry men ate the animals and used their skins for boats in which to cross the Snake.

78

A Pennsylvania Boyhood

An affectionate memoir of rural life a century ago

By JOHN NEWTON CULBERTSON

I was born August 22, 1841, in Amberson Valley, Franklin County, Pennsylvania. My ancestors migrated from Scotland to the north of Ireland soon after 1600 and emigrated from thence to America in 1712, settling in Chester, Pennsylvania. In 1729 they removed to what is now Franklin and named their settlement Culbertson's Row. They called themselves Scotch-Irish, a domineering race, aggressive, fearless, and tireless.

Amberson Valley, my birthland, lies snuggled between the Kittatinny and Tuscarora mountains: it is about four miles long and one mile wide, well watered, and originally was heavily wooded with oak, chestnut, hickory, sugar maple, and other trees. By the time I arrived on the scene, much of the timber had been cut away by the early settlers, some for building purposes, some for fencing and fuel. Much of it was wantonly destroyed. There was no market for timber at that date—every farmer had timber to burn, and the land was needed for farms.

The inhabitants of the valley were largely self-supporting. There was a sawmill that supplied all the lumber needed; a tannery that furnished an abundance of the best quality of leather for shoes, harnesses, and saddles; and there was a fuller in the valley who washed and whitened wool for weaving and spinning. The family looms wove quantities of cloth, called "linsey-woolsey." Maple sugar was in plenty; barley and rye were parched and used as a substitute for coffee. Almost every farmer cultivated a small patch of flax, in addition to corn, wheat, rye, and oats, and kept a few sheep; every housewife had her hackle for preparing flax for weaving, and a spinning wheel for transforming the beautiful fleecy wool into hanks of yarn. Many of the larger homes had looms on which the coarser fabrics called homespuns were woven. Among the first pictures in my mind is one of a couple of old ladies, sisters, bearing the quaint names of Leah and Diana, who lived in a little log cabin of two rooms, set in the stoniest part of the valley, and eked out a scanty living by weaving rugs and rag carpets for the neighbors. Often as a boy I sat by their loom and watched these skilled workers toss the shuttle back and forth with a peculiar jerk of the wrist. "My days are swifter than a weaver's shuttle."

In those days newspapers had limited circulation in rural districts, and as our valley was not on the line of general travel, news was at a premium. So when, in the early spring, the peddler with his pack would appear bringing news from the outside world and racy neighborhood gossip, which he would enlarge and decorate to suit his hearers' taste, his arrival was warmly greeted. In the fall he would come again, and at his heels would trail the cobbler, bearing his bag of awls, shoe lasts, and leather, together with his assortment of uncanny tales, folklore and ghost stories, the more improbable, the more readily believed.

The brook which flowed down the center of the valley furnished many quiet pools where good-sized fish lurked and, what was far better, "swimmin' holes," the joy of any boy.

In the mountains round the valley there was an abundance of game: deer, wild turkeys, squirrels, and rabbits. Foxes were too numerous for the safety of the barnyard fowl. There were birds galore. As the shadows of evening fell over the land, the melancholy whippoorwill set up his doleful cry, and in the spring great flocks of singing blackbirds would arrive.

The soil was very poor. Nature in one of her upheavals had covered the original limestone with several feet of gravel and rock, and the farmer had a weary task wringing support from the reluctant earth. The life of the housewife was extremely laborious and trying. In addition to such household cares as cooking, sweeping, scrubbing, washing, and ironing, she made the soap, milked the cows, fed the pigs and calves, cared for the chickens, ducks, turkeys, guinea hens, and geese; with the feathers of the last she filled her downy pillows and mattresses. Ofttimes I watched my mother, who, with a set look on her face, held the flapping, squawking goose with one hand and with her other hand plucked the soft white feathers. She made frocks for the girls, pants and coats for the boys, spun the yarn, and knit the socks and mittens for her family. Many times I was lulled to sleep by the soft hum of her spinning wheel or the click of her knitting needles. Most of my mother's sewing was done at night by the feeble light of a tallow dip. The tallow dip was for family use; the tallow candle was for use when "quality" called in after supper, or on some extra occasion.

The day began at 5 A.M. with breakfast. Prepared, precooked, predigested breakfast foods were not yet invented; bread, meat, potatoes, fruits, and coffee began the day. There was no end to the calls on the mother's time, strength, and ingenuity.

On Sunday afternoons Mother would read to us stories from the Bible, stories that never grew old. Part of an unseen yet real world, they were woven into the fabric of my life, and back of all was the word God, a word to be seriously spoken. Who was He? Where was He? My mother's answers were very discreet: "God is everywhere and always doing good." In my boyish mind I thought of God as grave and reverent, who sat by the side of a great opening at the roof of the sky and watched the world. He held in His hand a rod, with which He pointed out the places which His messengers should visit. With this vision I would fall to sleep in peace.

Many and wonderful were the ways in which fruits, —blackberries, huckleberries, gooseberries, plums, peaches, pears, grapes, and apples—were preserved for winter use. Sometimes I would be allowed to go down to the cellar and view the goodly storeroom where the winter supplies were kept; there were hanging shelves, whereon stood crocks in solemn array, looking as though they were conscious of their juicy contents. There were bins for potatoes, apples, turnips, and the fragrant onion; barrels of pickled beef, and rounds of carefully dried beef. There were hams, pork shoulders and flitches, which had been sugar-cured and then smoked with hickory wood, and corn cobs, hung in rows on hooks set in the sills of the floor overhead.

While the people in the valley were hard workers, they had their recreation. In the spring, summer, and fall there was little time for amusement, but in the winter season the young folks had sleighing parties; meeting in neighbors' houses for games and occasionally for dances; corn-husking parties on the barn floor, the happy finder of a red ear of corn being given the right to kiss the girl of his choice. The elderly women had their quilting parties, which furnished an admirable opportunity for social gossip. There were apple-butter boilings, where neighbors took turns stirring the fragrant apple juice, and in the early spring we tapped the sugar maples and boiled down the precious syrup.

The men had their raising bees, when the heavy timbers of houses and barns were put in place; the muster days, when the militia met for instruction and drill and just to have a good time generally. Road making and bridgebuilding were community work, and in mountain country brought the farmers together often.

The elderly people, I thought, had some queer notions. One was that boys should be kept busy to keep them out of mischief. My father displayed great ingenuity in his plans to keep me from idleness, such as picking up stones turned by the plow, or watching the sheep as they nibbled the grass on the commons along the foot of the mountain: sheep have no sense of location or direction; they were continually getting lost, and a lost sheep never finds the way home alone.

In the valley the farmers had two ways of thrashing out their small grain: the century-old way, treading it out by oxen and horses, or beating it out with the flail. When I reached the useful age, five years, I was set astride a quiet horse, the sheaves of grain were spread on the barn floor, and round and round the old horse walked, treading out the grain. Father stood by with a large wooden fork to shake up the straw at times. When I reached the age of eight, I was old enough to use the flail. You can get more exercise and less satisfaction out of half an hour's work with a flail than out of any other utensil invented by the ingenuity and skill of man.

In 1848 my father purchased a small threshing machine, the first in our section of the country. It was called a beater, I suppose because it beat the grain. The motive power was supplied by four horses. I remember standing off at a safe distance watching the thing start, and as I saw it going I realized that my occupation as a rider of the old horse that trod out the grain, and as an expert wielder of the romantic flail, was ended.

One of the early memories of my boyhood was the Mexican War. A young man, a near neighbor who often spent the evening at our home, enlisted early and was sent to Mexico. His death in Mexico was a matter of some importance to all of us at home.

I recall an incident in this connection. One evening my father came into the kitchen. A fire was burning in the wide chimney, and the weather was frosty. We young folks were gathered about the kitchen hearth, cracking nuts and scrapping as usual by the light of the fire, when Father came in and called to Mother, saying: "There must have been a big battle in Mexico today, as the sky in the southwest is so red."

I ran out of the house to look at the sky. The sun was going down, and lo, across the southwestern end of the valley the sun had hung great clouds, streamers of crimson with edgings of blue and gold. And as I looked at the startling sight, I wondered what a battle was like that could so color the heavens.

Then my father added that old people said that in the war of the Revolution, whenever a battle was fought, the sky was red over where the battle took place.

During my rest hours (and it seemed to me that I had

so few rest hours) I was set to study the shorter catechism. I had a very dim notion of what it was all about —I am not sure that I know yet—but my mother wanted me to learn it, and that was enough, so I kept on until I could repeat it without a miss.

After a lapse of fourscore years, I can still visualize the scene: An old-time kitchen, a wide fireplace and slumbering fire, a tallow dip for the light, a small, drowsy boy perched on a high stool by the kitchen table droning the words, a patient mother with book in hand helping him over the hard words.

I have witnessed many great scenes and pageants and memorable events in the course of a long life, yet most of them are but faint shadows on the canvas of memory, blurred by the years; but this lowly scene in all its original beauty abides in unchanging freshness.

The kitchen was a very important part of the house. Ours was a large room with a porch on the west and east sides. The north end of the room was taken up by a wide chimney, in which hung a crane for pots and kettles; a wide stone hearth lay in front of the fireplace. Much of the cooking was done in what were called Dutch ovens. A shovel of red-hot coals was raked out from the fireplace onto the hearth, the oven was set on the coals, the food was put

in the oven, the heavy iron lid was set on top, a shovel of hot coals put on the lid, and the baking process began.

Bread and pies were baked in an oven out of doors. A rough base about four feet square and three and a half feet high was built of stone and mortar. On top of this a circular dome was built, of smaller stones and mortar, three feet in diameter and eighteen inches high, with walls eight inches thick; on one side there was an opening a foot square. When the oven was needed for cooking, it was filled with wood and chips, which were set on fire and left burning until the fuel was consumed. Then the bread, pies, and cakes were put in, the oven door was securely fastened, and the baking began.

There was some folklore among the people, and a good deal of superstition. Very few had the hardihood to pass through the graveyard on a moonless night, lest they meet a ghost. Some believed that on very dark and stormy nights "graveyards did yawn and ghosts

did stalk forth." Rarely would a mother dare trim her baby's nails before he was a year old, for fear the child would become a thief.

One old woman in our neighborhood, of preternatural ugliness, was accused of bewitching the neighbors' cattle with two dread diseases, "hollow-horn" and "wolf-in-the-tail." In a nearby lonely cove in the mountain there was an old tumble-down house where years agone a man hanged himself; rumor said that the wretch's ghost was often seen at night sneaking about the ruined house with a rope in his hand.

Our section of the valley boasted a church building, the only one in the valley. It was built of logs, weatherboarded on the outside and plastered within, unpainted, without a particle of adornment. The windows had outside blinds, but I never saw them open; there was a center aisle; the men sat on the left side, the women on the right side. The preaching was of that virile type which left the sinner no loophole for escape. It was simply: Believe what I am telling you or be damned. There was reverence, seriousness, and sincerity. "Thus saith the Lord" was not lost on the hearers; it enabled men and women to smile at hardships, to do and endure. It was the preaching needed for that age.

I liked to go to church. There was in the quiet of the place, in the subdued manner of the people, a gentleness not apparent on weekdays, a toning down of the rough exterior. Everyone was in his best clothes and on his best behavior. The stress and haste of life were left outside for a time. The mind shared in the physical reaction and relief, and there fell on our souls a comforting sense of the reality and presence of the Infinite.

The church was also a public clearinghouse for information. Important news found easy circulation; it was a time and place for friendly intercourse, neighborhood gossip, and social reunions, where the cares and drudgery of the past week were forgotten.

The schoolhouse was a small affair, eighteen by twenty-four feet, built of logs and very roughly finished; at each end of the room there was a small window with six panes of glass. In the center of the room was a large, long stove. At one end of the room was the teacher's desk on which lay several good-sized rods of tough wood. These rods were for use, not ornament. The school directors went on the theory "Spare the rod, spoil the child." Seats for the scholars were arranged around the other three sides of the room. These seats were simply benches without backs, and were easily tipped over, which sometimes caused confusion. Our writing desks were long, wide boards fastened to the wall, extending round three sides of the room. The course of study was the three R's, administered in small doses. We were required to bring with us a copybook, a spelling book, a small arithmetic, and a copy of the New Testament—our school reader. Arithmetic was our terror; we never got beyond common fractions. The close of the school term of three months found most of us floundering in a bogmire of fractions.

There were many places of interest in the valley. The first of these was, in my mind, the old eagle's tree, as we called it. In an abandoned field at the foot of the mountain there was left standing a big tree, long since dead, which an old eagle had selected as his roosting place. Sometimes we boys would pay a visit to the field to catch a view of the eagle, but we were very careful not to venture beyond the fence that surrounded the field; we had been warned that eagles sometimes carried off small boys.

Another favorite spot was at the ford, where the road crossed the creek. A big log, flattened on one side for the use of foot passengers, was placed across the creek by the roadside. I remember this log very well. One day I was crossing the creek on the log when my dog ran by me and upset me into the water.

Up the creek was our neighborhood "swimmin' hole." It was a beautiful spot, out in the sunshine, and the pool had a sandy bottom. There was another spot on the road leading southward from our house where a small stream trickled across the roadway. Here from early spring till late fall was a trysting place for butterflies. Scores of the beautiful creatures flitted about, lazily fanning the air with their rainbow-colored wings.

All this and much more that cannot be framed in words—the intangible spirit of the field, the forest, the valley, and the mountains—we must leave be-

hind, for in the fall of 1849 my father was taken with a heavy case of "western fever." He caught the malady from his cousin, who had spent the summer of 1848 in Iowa and had made large investments in prairie lands. He was a good talker and easily persuaded my father that Iowa was the new land of promise, so our farm and all the stock was sold, our household goods were packed in wagons, good-byes were said, and we turned our faces toward the west.

Our means of transportation were two large covered wagons, each drawn by four stout horses. Room was reserved in one of the wagons for Mother and the smaller children. The larger children were booked to walk; thus we became part of that great caravan moving overland in the conquest of the West.

I well remember our start, on a Monday morning long before daylight. As our wagons rumbled down the valley, our old friends and neighbors called goodbye from their doorways and windows.

I was a boy of eight years, and this was the first great adventure of my life. I had had two sensational episodes in my life, but neither compared with the western journey.

When I was six years old my father took me with him on one of his trips over the mountains to the county town. I had often heard him speak of the train coming into the town, but I could not understand how the cars were drawn by a steam engine, so he promised me a trip to see for myself. One evening he told Mother to fix me up; he would take me along on the morrow.

It was my first journey away from home, and at starting the sensation was novel and enjoyable. But as we began to climb the mountains the familiar scenes were left behind and we passed out of sight of home. Then I regretted my journey. Oh, how I wished myself back home!

We reached our destination about noon and put up at the tavern for dinner. There was a porch in front. I waited on the porch until Father and the stableman put the horses away. In the meantime I peeked about. A large room opened onto the porch. On one side was the office; behind the office stood a line of shelves on which were arrayed, in rows, bottles big and little. I had never seen so many bottles in my life. Men came in, mostly countrymen, and called out to the clerk. He would reach up, take a bottle from the shelf, and pour some of its contents into dirty glasses. The men swallowed the liquid with a grimace, as though the stuff were unpalatable, and wiped their mouths with the backs of their hands. Then they would go to a corner of the room where there was a tin basin grimy with dirt, pour some water into the basin, wash their hands and faces, and dry off with a towel dirtier than the basin. They looked robust, healthy; maybe dirt agreed with them.

The dinner bell rang and Father took me into the dining room. The men nearly knocked me down in the rush; they seemed to be in a hurry—ate in a hurry, talked in a hurry, walked in a hurry. I did not enjoy my dinner; the food didn't taste like the dinners at home. I was glad when it was over.

After dinner Father took me out to see the cars. As we passed down the street, we crossed a small stream on a large stone bridge. By the bridge there was a water wheel, which was turned by the stream that flowed under the bridge. I told Father to stop, I wanted to see the wheel go round. We stopped a few minutes. I was fascinated by the wheel, every detail was impressed on my memory. We went on to see the railroad cars, but I hardly saw them, they made no mark on my mind; the water wheel had filled every corner and nook of my little head.

At 3 P.M., to my joy, we started homeward. It was late when we arrived. Mother had placed a dim light in the kitchen window that looked toward the road. The next day I began work on a small water wheel like the one I had seen in town; when it was finished I set it running in a little rivulet that crossed the road a short distance below our house.

The fall of 1848 furnished another adventure. One evening at dusk Father called to Mother to gather the children into the house at once and keep them in. This was an unheard-of thing, but Mother corralled her troop in the kitchen; it was cool and there was a glowing fire in the wide, open fireplace. After dark Father came in and explained what had happened.

That evening just before dark Father had discovered five Negroes, one woman and four men, hiding in the orchard; they were runaway slaves, on their way from the South to Canada. I subsequently learned that this was not my parents' first venture in keeping a station on the once famous underground railroad.

After Father and Mother had a talk, they prepared a basket of food and a jug of water and carried it to the barn for the fugitives. The folks had just gotten back from the barn, and we were all talking about the strange adventure, when we heard a loud hello at the pump by the roadside west of the house, perhaps twenty feet from the kitchen.

Father went out to answer the call. I sneaked out to hear what was going on; my father, seeing me, gave me a ringing cuff on the ear, and sent me back to the house. I went back and sat down on the porch, but my ears were sharp and I heard the whole story. These creatures, the two men at the pump, were hunting the five runaways. The fact was, although I did not know it then, that Captain Culbertson's house was marked by the "slave catchers." The owners of runaway slaves would frequently advertise the loss of their slaves, giving descriptions and offering rewards for their capture; and sad to say, there were men on the border low-down enough to pursue and sometimes capture the poor wretches.

The first words spoken were startling. "Captain, we are chasing five runaway Negroes. We have traced them to this neighborhood. Have you seen anything of them?" There was a silence for a moment, and then Father said: "Well, Jim, if I had I would not tell you. You don't think that I would help you in your dirty business? If that is all you want to see me about, you might as well move on." Jim and his unsavory partner moved on.

That night about midnight the runaways were piloted by my father up to the head of the valley and given directions about how to move onward on the mysterious underground railway that led toward freedom. This was the last chapter of my parents' connection with the underground system. The situation was becoming dangerous. In one of the parties of slaves who passed through our hands was a sick woman who could no longer keep up with her companions; she was cared for by Mother until she was able to go forward on her difficult journey.

But as I have said, the trip to the new West was the third and greatest of my boyhood sensations. The only shadow that marred the fair scene was that Mother did not seem herself. I could not fathom the cause then. I know now; all her life had its roots here. Here she was born, here she was married, here her children were born, here dwelt her kinsfolk, the strong, far-reaching ties of blood and friendships. Here she had borne the heat and the burden; now, when the shadows were beginning to lengthen, all must be put behind her, and in a strange land a new beginning must be made.

Toward evening of the first day we reached Fort Loudon at the foot of the valley, on the Baltimore and Pittsburgh pike, then the great highway from the East to Pittsburgh. Here were long trains of covered wagons, and great coaches, drawn by six horses, carrying mail and passengers. To me, a boy raised in the quiet of the country, it was a wonderful sight to watch the great coaches whirl by, raising clouds of dust, the driver so skillfully guiding the swiftly moving horses. Had I been able to drive a six-horse coach, my boyish ambition would have been fully satisfied.

Every day was full of excitement—new scenes, new faces. It was circus and movie, two in one, in real life, nothing made up. Many of the gentlemen in the coaches wore high white collars, great silk stocks, high stiff hats, rich blue shad-bellied coats adorned with highly polished brass buttons. The ladies had great poke bonnets; I cannot describe their garments. At the posthouses, the "quality" dined in a separate room and had waiters; we common folks ate in the ordinary dining room and helped ourselves. Mother and the children slept in the posthouses; Father slept in the wagon to care for the stuff.

All went well until we reached the Allegheny Mountains; here we had some real excitement. A driving snowstorm came down on the mountain unexpectedly, a month too soon. The wind blew straight into the faces of the drivers. The rule of the road was that the teams ascending should have the right of way. When the storm was at its worst, we met teams coming down the mountain, and for some reason they refused to give way. Hades broke loose, epithets were hurled back and forth, two or three men stripped for the fray, vow-

ing they would pitch each other down the mountainside. But soon the storm diminished in severity, the gentlemen who had shed their coats put them on again, the train descending the mountain gave way, and our caravan moved on up the mountain. After this incident, our journey was without any untoward event.

Our caravan reached Pittsburgh on a Saturday afternoon. Next morning we and our chattels were dumped on board a steamer bound for St. Louis. As we drove down through the city to the steamboat landing, I noticed that the boys, who were on their way to Sunday school, wore short pants reaching just below the knees and long stockings. I called Mother's attention to it, and asked if that was the right way for boys to dress.

There were many strange sights and stranger sounds. We passed a church; the doors were open, and someone was playing an organ. I did not know then what an organ was. I only knew that something within me responded to the stirring chords. I was accustomed to the music of the violin, but the tones of the organ sent their plummet down into the deeper soundings of the soul. I had crossed the threshold of a new world.

The steamers of those days were built with an eye to the needs of the great body of immigrants then moving west, to give comfortable accommodations at a price within their means for themselves and their stock. On the lower deck toward the stern of the boat, suites of rooms were fitted up in simple fashion, with a large stove outside where all the families could prepare their meals.

In the center of the boat, just forward and adjoining the family section, stalls were prepared for horses and cattle, and sties for pigs. There were coops for chickens, crates for ducks and geese.

There was a family of three, quartered near our rooms, who talked all the time, all at once, and their voices were pitched in a shrieking key. With this trio was an old man. He was among them, but not of them. Rather tall and spare, he wore old-fashioned clothing; he had come out of the past, a "relic of a bygone age." My father learned that he had been a soldier of the American Revolution, and he took my brother William and myself to see the elderly soldier. The old gentleman lived in the twilight memories of the past; he talked freely of his services under Washington, Greene, and Mad Anthony Wayne.

The sight of the old soldier awakened my boyish interest. In my mind, I could imagine myself marching by his side to the shrill notes of the fife and the blood-stirring drumbeat on the battlefields of Lexington and Trenton, of Camden and Yorktown. It was as though a voice had called me saying, "Be ready, I may need you."

On our arrival at St. Louis, we boarded another steamer bound for Iowa and St. Paul, Minnesota. The accommodations on the second steamer were similar to those on the first, but we were among a new set of travellers. There were not so many now, so we had more space; the old soldier and the trio of clamoring foghorns had disembarked at St. Louis.

As we moved northward from St. Louis, the weather grew cooler. The month was waning, and as we neared the end of our long journey our spirits rose. The older folks talked of plans for the new life in the new land. We reached Princeton, Iowa, at noon on a day in late October, 1849. The day was warm, sunshine welcomed our party to Iowa. Wagons were on hand to carry us and our household goods to our new home seven miles west.

It was well toward evening when all were ready to start. After we had been on the way a few miles, the weather suddenly changed, the wind veered to the northwest, a biting blast beat in our faces; winter was showing her teeth early. Night overtook us before we reached our destination.

Mother begged the driver to stop at the first house, which proved to be a small sod dugout of two rooms, occupied by a frontiersman, his wife, two children, and three dogs. The fire was stirred up and we soon thawed out, ready for another attempt to reach our destination, which we did in a short time.

Our new home was a large stone building, erected without any regard for convenience or comfort. Our bedding was spread on the floor for the first night's rest in what was to be our home for four eventful years. Here my eldest brother and sister both were married; here my second eldest sister entered on that long, final, mysterious journey, and here a brother and two sisters were added to the family circle.

The day after our arrival broke fair, and we children were out taking an inventory of our surroundings. On the north, a perfectly level plain stretched out to a small river, bordered by a belt of timber, three miles distant. On the south, rolling prairies, utterly treeless, extended for several miles; we had but one neighbor within three miles. Game was abundant, herds of antelope and deer were in sight almost any hour of the day; wild geese and ducks, prairie chickens, grouse, and quail were plentiful.

In the evening about sundown our play was interrupted by our mother, who came running toward us calling, "Look at the wolves." We turned to look in the direction of the fence a few rods away, and there to our horror were perhaps half a dozen gray wolves glaring at us through the fence. At the appearance of our mother and our two elder sisters, the wolves trotted away.

A few days after our arrival in Iowa we were treated to a sight magnificent but fearsome, a prairie on fire. Just before dusk one evening we noticed great clouds of smoke darkening the western sky, and as night came on we were startled and frightened at the sight of a long line of fire moving toward us, driven by a westerly wind. The sight was majestic beyond anything to be seen on earth, and yet terrifying; the low, cringing, creeping flame, then the sudden leaping high in the air of great fiery tongues, sputtering, hissing, snapping.

The prairie was covered with a heavy crop of dry grass, much of it two feet high; there was nothing to stop the onward rush of the fire save half a dozen small farmhouses and outbuildings which were protected by strips of plowed land, about a rod wide, called firebreaks.

It was a new thing in our lives. We folks stood spellbound for a time, not fully aware of the danger that menaced our home. But while we were hesitating and debating just what to do, our nearest neighbor, he of the sod dugout, came hurrying up to our house, calling on the men to get out the plows, and the women and children to get old bags and blankets and buckets of water and fight the fire, or we would all be burned out of house and home.

What a wild rush for the next few minutes! Our neighbor led the procession. There was an old firebreak around our place. The plowmen soon were turning this over again. The women and children were stationed along the newly plowed strip with buckets of water and bags. Backfires were kindled at many places; our work was to prevent the backfire from sneaking across the plowed ground. This did happen in some cases, and vigilance was needed.

On came the devouring flood of flame and the smothering clouds of smoke, but when it reached the slowly creeping backfire, it died down and perished in a moment. The great flames swept by on either side, but we were safe.

The year 1851 was the year noted for the great flocks of carrier pigeons that infested the country. It was seeding time in the spring when tens of thousands of pigeons invaded the country. Where they came from, no one knew. After a few weeks they disappeared, and where they went, no one knew. Our small grains were sown by hand, and the birds followed the sower, devouring the grains as fast as they were sown; so numerous and so tame were they that we could kill them with a stick.

The pigeons were not the only enemies we had to fight in the seeding season. Gophers, chipmunks, and ground squirrels drove us to the verge of madness in corn-planting time. The field for corn was carefully prepared; long, straight, shallow furrows were made across the field in two directions at right angles, and the seed corn was dropped three or four grains at a time, just where the furrows crossed each other. A man followed the dropper and covered the seed corn with soft, mellow dirt and then pressed the dirt firm with his foot.

Now it is hard to believe, but those gophers and ground squirrels caught on to the footmark in no time. On the second day, when we reached the field to continue our corn planting, we were amazed to find the little devils had followed the furrows and wherever there was the pressure of the shoe, there they had dug up the seed corn and eaten the heart out of it. Fully one-half of the first day's planting had been eaten. Our corn planting was finally completed with success, but it took us a long time to rid the fields of the pests.

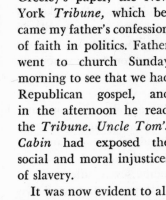

ILLUSTRATED FOR AMERICAN HERITAGE BY W. KIRKMAN PLUMMER

The year of 1852 was a year of great political excitement. It was worse than the visits of the pigeons, or the squirrel and gopher pests of 1851.

The question of slavery was discussed heatedly. A book called *Uncle Tom's Cabin* furnished fuel for the fire. In November, 1852, my father took a load of voters to the polls, seven miles distant. General Winfield Scott of Mexican fame, the last candidate of the Whigs, on that day went down to defeat. It was late in the afternoon before my father succeeded in getting his voters back into the wagon: too much Iowa corn juice. The old Whig banner was folded, never to float to victory again. As we rode home I could hear the older men predicting a storm and a bloody outcome.

On the breakup of the Whig party, the Republican party was organized, and my father joined it. In the campaign of 1856, John C. Frémont was its candidate. Slavery was all the talk. In addition to the county papers my father took Horace Greeley's paper, the New York *Tribune*, which became my father's confession of faith in politics. Father went to church Sunday morning to see that we had Republican gospel, and in the afternoon he read the *Tribune*. *Uncle Tom's Cabin* had exposed the social and moral injustices of slavery.

It was now evident to all that America had reached the end of the old road; freedom and slavery could no longer walk together.

In the fall of 1858 a great comet appeared in the western skies, and dire were the prophecies. For weeks it moved across the sky, a gleaming head with a great fan-shaped train. As we watched it from our front yard, strange weird thoughts were in our minds.

When, inevitably, the war came, John Culbertson was living in the mining town of Cripple Creek, Colorado; he walked all the way to Leavenworth, Kansas, to enlist in a cavalry regiment, in which he served for four years. He was badly wounded but recovered and became a Presbyterian missionary, first in South Dakota, afterward in Siam. There he met and married a lady missionary, Miss Belle Caldwell, and it was to their son, John, that the old man dictated this memoir nearly forty years ago. It was sent to AMERICAN HERITAGE *by the younger Culbertson and his wife, Edna, of Salt Lake City.*

The Case of the Plodding Highwayman CONTINUED FROM PAGE 53

He opened it, found that the barrels were clean and bright, and observed to its owner that it was a good weapon.

Bart smiled. "It always gets what I go after. I never waste ammunition. I save money in other ways, too," he said. "I don't drink or smoke."

Then he asked what he owed his host for the hospitality. It was a somewhat peculiar question in a pioneer territory, where a stranger was welcomed as a guest. Shortridge courteously refused payment, but Bart couldn't let it go at that. "Did you ever hear," he said with a sudden smile, "of Black Bart?"

"Hear of him!" Shortridge cried. "He's one of the main things talked about in these parts nowadays."

"Well," said Bart, "I'm Black Bart. I just thought that if you knew who I am, you might be willing to accept something for your kindness."

The logger thought he was joking. "Sure you ain't Joaquín Murrieta, or some other tough hombre we all thought was planted safe under the dirt?"

Bart didn't take the joshing at all kindly. His sense of humor never did work when someone made fun of him. The smile disappeared, Shortridge recalled years later, and the jaw muscles hardened as he repeated his identity in sepulchral tones. This time Shortridge got the full voltage, and he drew a long breath and shakily thanked Bart for not telling him on the previous evening and spoiling a good night's sleep. There had been no danger, Bart said; he had never harmed a soul. Then he added something that stuck in Shortridge's mind for over three years before he realized what it meant: "You'd feel easier if I told you some other things, but it would be too risky."

The thing Bart couldn't risk revealing was that he held up stages with an empty gun. Shortridge recalled later that not only was Bart's shotgun empty when he examined it, but not even one of his guest's pockets was lumpy with shells. Bart himself was quoted after his capture as saying that "the moral effect" of a shotgun was sufficient for his purposes.

He was right on this point twenty-six times out of twenty-eight. The first time the bluff failed was on July 13, 1882, when a plucky shotgun messenger took a chance and fired in Bart's general direction. The driver of the stage immediately cracked his whip and the horses plunged ahead, bowling Bart to one side and leaving him sprawled in the road. It was his only utter fiasco—perhaps because he made the mistake of trying to hold up a stage on the thirteenth day of the month.

The second time that his unloaded gun failed of its full moral effect occurred sixteen months later, in November of 1883, and that turned out to be his last holdup. The stage he planned to rob was the one that ran between Sonora and Milton—by some coincidence (dare we call it poetic justice?) the very same one he had knocked off on his premier holdup. First Bart headed for Tuttletown, California, where at irregular intervals a stage picked up amalgam from Patterson gold mine. By making friends and keeping his eyes and ears open, Bart found out that the next shipment was scheduled for November 3.

He then set off on foot and walked most of the route the stage would take, to find the best place for a holdup. (Notice the patient, plodding technique—the minute re-examination of an already familiar road.) He decided on a spot a mile from his first holdup. Then, a few days before the shipment was due, he hiked higher into the mountains and set up camp, with a good view of the road below. His gear included field glasses to follow the course of the stage and a watch to time it with; his usual camp fare of coffee, crackers, and sugar; a pot in which to boil creek water; matches and a knife; two pairs of detachable cuffs; his bedroll; his flour-sack-and-duster disguise; a shotgun; and an axe.

Two or three days before the shipment was to be made, he established an observation post quite near the road. His strategy was by now routine: to step out into the road as the stage came thundering along; aim his shotgun at the driver's heart; shield himself by standing in front of one of the lead horses as the stage squealed to a halt; and call out in his hollow voice, "Throw down the box." Then, after sending the stage on its way again, he would chop open the express-company box, scoop up the valuables, and leave—at once and on foot.

But this time a little thing went wrong. A nineteen-year-old youth, one Jimmy Rolleri, had hitched a ride with the stage driver, and Jimmy had a gun. If he had stayed on the stage, Bart could have handled him, but Jimmy was hunting small game that day, and he got off the stage, intending to take a shortcut over the hill and catch up with it again on the other side.

Bart had seen this passenger through his field glasses and was rattled a bit when the stage arrived at the ambush without him. The driver told him the truth—that the boy had got off to hunt small game—but Bart's timing was then thrown off a little more because Wells Fargo had recently decided to bolt their express boxes to the floors of the stages. Rather than waste time getting this one unbolted, Bart ordered the driver to unhitch the horses and take them up the road a piece while he himself climbed inside the stage and hacked open the box. He had got the treasure out and was already running for the woods when it happened.

The boy with the gun had found the driver standing with the unhitched team, and the two crept up on the stage and opened fire on the fleeing road agent. Bart was winged, but the main damage was not to his person but to his performance. As he scuttled away

REWARD!

WELLS, FARGO & CO.'S EXPRESS BOX, CON-
taining $160 in Gold Notes, was robbed this morning, by one man, on the route from Sonora to Milton, near top of the Hill, between the river and Copperopolis.

$250

And one-fourth of any money recovered, will be paid for arrest and conviction of the robber.

JOHN J. VALENTINE,

San Francisco, July 27, 1875.   General Sup't.

At the height of Bart's career, it was rumored that the rewards for his capture totalled as much as $18,000. The truth must have hurt Bart's pride: they never added up to more than $800, part of it offered in this Wells Fargo poster.

into the brush, he dropped things: his derby, his crackers and sugar, the case for his field glasses. Of all the miscellany he left behind, only one item proved a good clue, and it was as prosaic a clue as one could imagine—a handkerchief with the laundry mark F.X.O.7.

About six months earlier, Detective Hume had hired a special operative, Harry N. Morse, to spend all his time running Black Bart to earth. Now, with the laundry-marked handkerchief in his hand, Morse knew that he was finally closing in. By great good luck he began his search in San Francisco, where Black Bart was then living under the name of C. E. Bolton, supposedly a prosperous mining man—which, in a second-hand way, he was.

Morse ran the laundry mark down in a week, located Bart at a lodging house at 37 Second Street, and it was all over but the confession. Bart held out for three days, standing on his dignity, feigning outrage at being questioned, and even inventing an instant

new alias, "T. Z. Spaulding." Nevertheless, he was booked on suspicion of stage robbery, and when the authorities took him back to the holdup area and people began recalling him as having just been seen there, he cracked. By moonlight he led Morse and the local lawmen to a rotting log in which he had cached the gold amalgam—$4,200 worth—and told them everything they wanted to know.

In return for his co-operation Bart got a light sentence—six years, based on his confession to the one holdup. He became Prisoner No. 11,046 in San Quentin Prison on November 21, 1883, only eighteen days after his last stage robbery. With time off for good behavior, he was a free man once again on January 21, 1888, having served four years and two months.

As Black Bart the Po8 he was still news. A reporter sent to interview him upon his release asked whether he had any more poetry to give out. The years behind bars had not destroyed Boles' sense of humor. He replied with a grin: "Young man, didn't you just hear me say I will commit no more crimes?"

Nor did he, so far as is known, though for a while Hume suspected him of two holdups that occurred later that year. Nevertheless, two more poems were linked to old Bart's name. One was produced by a newspaper man in the mining country, who tried to palm it off as Bart's work:

> *So here I've stood while wind and rain*
> *Have set the trees a-sobbin'*
> *And risked my life for that damned stage*
> *That wasn't worth the robbin'.*

The other verse connected with his name was a long, rambling affair written by Ambrose Bierce, then running a column in the San Francisco *Examiner*, as a comment on Bart's prison-release news conference. The most memorable stanza was this:

> *What's that?—you ne'er again will rob a stage?*
> *What! did you so? Faith, I didn't know it.*
> *Was that what threw poor Themis in a rage?*
> *I thought you were convicted as a poet!*

Black Bart's poetry may have lacked Bierce's classical allusions, but it scanned better.

Ken and Pat Kraft are a husband-and-wife writing team from Carmel, California. They ran across Black Bart in old California newspaper files while living in Santa Rosa, doing research for their seventh book, a biography of Luther Burbank to be published soon by Appleton-Century.

For further reading: Wild Oats in Eden, *by Harvey J. Hansen and Jeanne Thurlow Miller (Hooper, Santa Rosa, 1962);* Wells Fargo, *by Edward Hungerford (Random House, 1949);* Bad Company, *by Joseph Henry Jackson (Harcourt, Brace, 1949).*

Ordeal in Hell's Canyon

CONTINUED FROM PAGE 78

it was the start of a breakdown of discipline and morale that would lead eventually to Hunt's loss of control over the men.

Remaining in the canyon with the rest of the party, Hunt buried the company's baggage and equipment in caches and tried unsuccessfully to increase the supply of food by catching fish or beaver. After several days, Crooks's group and two of Reed's men straggled back to camp. The former reported that the travel by land back to Henry's huts had been so slow and disheartening that they had abandoned the attempt. Reed's men were equally discouraging. They had found neither Indians nor food on the route ahead, and had turned back when Reed and the fourth member of their party, arguing that they could be of no help to Hunt, had insisted on pressing ahead.

Hunt and his companions were now alarmed. Winter was approaching rapidly, and none of them knew how far they still had to go, or what mountains and other perils were still ahead of them. But to remain where they were would mean certain starvation. Deciding to follow the direction of McClellan and Reed, the men divided into two bands, to give each one a better chance of survival, and on November 9 started forward on foot along opposite rims of the canyon. Ramsay Crooks, with nineteen men, proceeded down the south side, and Hunt, with twenty-two others, including Marie Dorion and her two children, followed the north rim. The hardy Iowa woman, well advanced in pregnancy, carried a two-year-old on her back and led a four-year-old by the hand, keeping up with the men without a murmur of weariness. The total food supply for all forty-three people, divided between the two groups before they separated, amounted to forty pounds of dried corn, twenty pounds of grease, about five pounds of bouillon tablets, and enough dried meat to allot each person five and a half pounds.

Day after day, the Astorians struggled along through the sagebrush and lava-scarred wastes of the Snake plains, using up their food and suffering from thirst. The river was always below them, but, except on rare occasions, they were unable to make their way down the canyon walls to its banks. The members of Crooks's party were reduced to eating the soles of their moccasins. Hunt's group, lagging behind, finally came on an Indian trail that led them to a miserable straw-hut settlement of impoverished and frightened Shoshonis. The Indians traded them some dried salmon and a dog to eat, and the travellers continued on, passing similar wickiup camps of Shoshonis whose small offerings of food served to keep them alive, but did little to ease their hunger. At length they found Indians with horses and were able to bargain for several animals, on one of which they placed Dorion's wife. Almost due south of present-day Boise, they took the advice of an Indian and, leaving the Snake River, turned north, plodding across a seemingly endless desert and almost dying of thirst. Some of the Canadians in anguish had begun to drink their urine before the party finally reached the banks of the Boise River, near the site of Idaho's future capital city.

Following the Boise to its mouth, they arrived back on the Snake River and moved along it again as it flowed north through barren hills toward a formidable range of mountains capped with snow. At the entrance to a narrow passage where the river began to force its way through steep and rugged basalt cliffs, they paused among another band of Shoshonis, learning from them that white men, travelling on both sides of the river, had preceded them into the canyon. Hunt was cheered to know that Crooks and probably McClellan and Reed were safely ahead of him, and his spirits were roused further when Indians told him that after three sleeps in the mountains, he would meet another nation of people whom they called the Sciatogas, and that from the homes of those people it was only six more sleeps to the falls of the Columbia River.

The Sciatogas were Cayuses and Nez Perces who often raided the Shoshonis from the north, and the wild and dark defile into which Hunt's people hopefully plunged on November 29 was the forbidding Grand Canyon of the Snake River, the deepest gorge on the North American continent (7,900 feet deep at its maximum)—and to this day one of the least accessible in the United States. No white man had yet been through this awesome mountain trench, which now forms part of the border between Oregon and Idaho, and no one who had known its extent of more than 100 miles would have tried forcing it in winter. But Hunt was unaware of its dangers, and he was in difficulty almost at once. The narrow benchland along the water, hemmed by walls that rose thousands of feet above him, became rocky and impassable, and Hunt tried to climb the cliff. The steep route was dizzying, and the travellers, already weak from hunger, moved along perilous ledges and basalt rimrock, edging close to the cliffsides to keep from falling. On the heights, "so high," wrote Hunt, "that I would never have believed our horses could have got over them," they ran into a snowstorm that "fell so densely on the mountains where we had to go that we could see nothing a half-mile ahead."

At an earlier season they might have gotten through the canyon. But winter had struck, and they were now to pay dearly for their previous delays and false hopes. One whole day they were unable to move in the storm, and remained encamped, eating one of the horses they had traded from the Shoshonis and shivering in the bitter cold. When the weather cleared, they had a dismaying view of the country ahead of them—range upon range of mountains, all covered with snow and extending as far as they could see. They made only a few miles a day, returning occasionally to the river, but climbing again when the dark canyon walls rose close to the water and barred their progress. On December 4, they floundered in snow that came above their knees. The cold dulled their minds and made them sleepy, and on one occasion, Hunt noted, they escaped what seemed a sure death only by coming on a clump of pines that gave them the makings of a roaring fire. The next day the snowfall cut visibility to three hundred yards, and they returned again to the river, slipping and sliding down a rocky slope through a fog that obscured the bottom of the canyon. On December 6, when the fog cleared, they were startled to see a party of men coming through the gorge toward them, but on the opposite side of the river. It was Crooks's group, so wasted from hunger that Hunt scarcely recognized any of them. They stood on the rocks, calling hoarsely across the stream for food, and Hunt had a boat hastily made from the skin of a horse that they had butchered the night before, and sent some meat across to them.

The boat returned with Crooks and one of his men, a Canadian named François LeClerc, who, weak-voiced and scarcely able to stand up unassisted, told Hunt that they had struggled three days farther down the river. There, near the most awesome part of the chasm, the narrowest and most rugged section, since that time given the name Hell's Canyon, the rock walls had been so close together and the river so wild and frightening that they had climbed with difficulty to the mountain top, where the view of the snow-covered wilderness, still extending as far as they could see, had appalled them. Realizing that they could

John Jacob Astor

never get through alive, they had turned back in the hope of finding help before starvation overtook them.

They also had news of the other groups. Several days before their worst trials had begun, they had sighted the parties of Reed and Donald McKenzie trudging downriver along the opposite shore. The burly McKenzie had called across to them that McClellan's men were also heading north, following a route farther east, which they thought would lead them to the land of the Flathead Indians.

Hunt had persevered bravely, but the end seemed to have been reached. Discouraged by Crooks's report, he determined to turn the whole party around and get out of the terrifying mountains before they all died. During the night, the skin boat was swept away by the current, and the next day an attempt to ferry Crooks and LeClerc back across the stream with some meat for their men failed when a hastily constructed raft proved unmanageable in the torrent. There was no time to build another craft. Now that the men knew they were going back, out of the canyon, they were impatient to start moving, and Hunt finally ordered the two parties to travel abreast of each other on opposite sides of the river. At first the enfeebled Crooks and LeClerc managed to keep up, but their strength soon gave out, and they began to hold up Hunt's group. As the pace slowed, some of the men became panicky and urged Hunt to abandon Crooks. Hunt refused to do so, but could not prevent his party from breaking up as some men, alone or in small groups, slipped away from him. Desperate to save themselves before it was too late, they hurried southward along the rushing river and over the ledges on the canyon walls.

For a while, Hunt and several of his men continued to assist Crooks and LeClerc. But, finally, it was evident that everyone would perish unless Hunt hurried on and found an Indian village where he could secure food to send back to the starving men. He pushed ahead and, after existing for two days on a solitary beaver skin, came suddenly on a band of Shoshonis who had descended from the mountains to camp along the river. He had meanwhile overtaken the rest of his men; and the sight of so many strangers appearing unexpectedly from the direction of the homeland of their Nez Perce enemies terrified the Shoshonis, who fled in fright, leaving some of their horses behind them. The weakened men managed to catch five of the animals and, after making a meal of one of them, sent a mounted messenger back to Crooks and LeClerc with a supply of meat. The food arrived in time, and shortly afterward they appeared at Hunt's camp.

An attempt was now made to feed the starving men of Crooks's original band, who had arrived on the op-

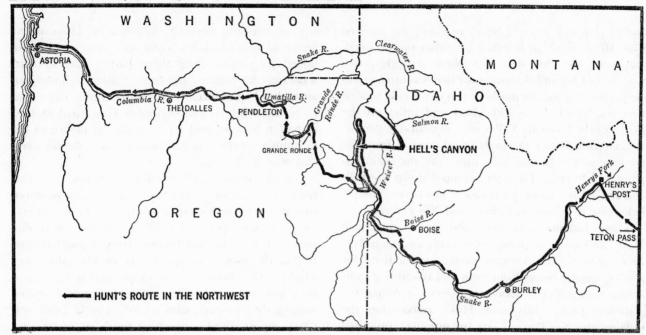

← HUNT'S ROUTE IN THE NORTHWEST

posite shore of the river. Another crude boat was made from the skin of a horse, and the food was ferried over to them. On a second trip across the turbulent water, one of Crooks's men, crazed by his suffering, jumped into the craft and, clapping his hands and leaping about in delirium, upset the skin boat. While the others watched in horror, he was swept away by the current and drowned.

When the men's hunger was appeased, the disheartened parties set off again, continuing their doleful retreat from the mountains. Crooks was still too weak to travel; and a Canadian, Jean Baptiste Dubreuil, and a tall, forty-year-old Virginia frontiersman named John Day, who were also too emaciated and feeble to keep up with the rest, stayed behind with him, hoping to regain their strength and eventually catch up with the expedition. The rest of Hunt's men hastened south and on December 16, after three weeks in the canyon, emerged from the mountains and camped near the lodges of a band of Shoshonis on Idaho's Weiser River.

The Shoshonis were surprised to see them and told them that they could never have gotten all the way through the canyon. The information made Hunt worry about the fate of Donald McKenzie and the other men whom Crooks had sighted along the river. The Shoshonis also revealed that there was another, more westerly route to the country of the Sciatogas and the Columbia River; but since it too crossed mountains, it would be unwise to take it at this time of the year. Hunt was impatient to be off, however, and after many pleas and threats, he secured three Indians as guides and ferried his men across the Snake River in a boat made of two skins. Three French Canadians de-

cided to remain among the Shoshonis, where there was at least some food and the possibility of trapping, but they promised to try to find Crooks and his two companions and eventually make their way with them to the Columbia River. On December 24, Hunt and his men again struck off overland, following an Indian route that led northwest from the country of the Shoshonis to the Grande Ronde Valley of northeastern Oregon. That part of the journey was to be of considerable significance, for it amounted to the discovery by white men of a feasible, short-cut route between the Snake River country of southern Idaho and the Columbia River. In Hunt's wake, trappers, traders, and other travellers came to use it regularly, and in time it became an important leg of the famous Oregon Trail.

The Astorians' hardships, however, were not ended. For several days they travelled through rain and snow, crossing cold, blustery plains and high hills; and another Canadian, Michel Carriere, gave up and had to be left behind. On December 30, near the Grande Ronde Valley, Marie Dorion, still plodding along with the others, paused to give birth to her baby. The Dorion family waited with her, while the rest of the party pushed ahead. The next day, the doughty woman and her family caught up, and Hunt wrote in his journal that the Indian mother "was on horseback with her newborn infant in her arms; another, aged two years, wrapped in a blanket, was slung at her side. One would have said, from her air, that nothing had happened to her."

In the Grande Ronde, a great oval valley of rich grass and marshland, the party came on a small camp of Shoshonis. They lingered with them only briefly, and on January 2, 1812, began to climb the forested Blue Mountains that hemmed the valley on the north and west. After five days of renewed struggle across wooded heights and through snow that was often waist-deep, they reached the northern rim of the cold wilderness and gazed down with cheer and relief on the plains of the Umatilla Valley near present-day Pendleton, Oregon. Before the party could descend from the mountains, the Dorion baby died, and the Astorians paused to bury it. Then they trooped down the hills and arrived at a sprawling village of mat-covered lodges belonging to a band of Cayuses and Nez Perces.

These Indians were bold and picturesque, said Hunt, and possessed huge horse herds and abundant food supplies. The Astorians rested among them for a week, buying horses from them and rebuilding their strength on a diet of roots and deer meat. When the travellers pushed off again, Hunt, considering the Cayuses and Nez Perces likely fur suppliers, promised to send men back to them to trade for beaver skins.

The worst of the journey was now over. Moving down the Umatilla Valley, the party finally reached the Columbia on January 21, 1812. It was, wrote Hunt, "for so long the goal of our desires. We had traveled 1,751 miles, we had endured all the hardships imaginable. With difficulty I expressed our joy at sight of this river." The group crossed the Columbia to follow a trail along the northern shore, and near the present-day city of The Dalles took to canoes. On February 12, 1812, without further mishap, Hunt's men reached the Columbia's mouth to find that the members of the sea group had arrived almost a full year earlier, in March, 1811, and had built a post which they had named Fort Astor, or Astoria.

In a happy climax to his arrival, Hunt also found eleven of his own men at the fort. They were the members of the parties of McKenzie, McClellan, and Reed, who had preceded Crooks and himself into the great canyon of the Snake. Exhausted and in rags, they had reached the mouth of the Columbia on January 18, almost a month ahead of Hunt, and they, too, had a

story of hardship to relate. After leaving Hunt on the Snake plains, where the combined group had abandoned its canoes, their three parties had searched separately for Indians and food. Failing to find assistance, they had eventually encountered each other and, rather than return and encumber Hunt, had decided to hasten forward and try to reach the mouth of the Columbia, where they had hoped to find the sea party and send back help.

Led by the bold and herculean McKenzie, they had trudged across the plains that bordered the northern edge of the Snake, suffering painfully from hunger and thirst. At some point, possibly just below the confluence of the Snake and Weiser rivers in southwestern Idaho, the men had apparently decided that they would have a better chance of survival if they again split into smaller groups and took different routes. Seeking the Flatheads, who, according to the Lewis and Clark report, lived somewhere north of where they then were, McClellan and several men had left the Snake and had climbed northeastward over the mountains.

Two groups under McKenzie and Reed had continued into the great canyon, but after a while they too had climbed the mountains and had run again into McClellan's party along the divide between the Snake and the Weiser. Together once more, they had traversed rugged country for twenty-one days, urged on by McKenzie's aggressive determination, and living solely on five beavers and two mountain goats that they had shot. During the last five days of their struggle through the high wilderness, they had existed entirely on the skins of the beavers. Finally, they had descended to the Little Salmon River, where they had come on some wild horses, a few of which they had managed to kill for food. Shortly afterward, they had reached the main Salmon River and settlements of friendly Nez Perce Indians, who had given them camas roots and other food and had guided them to the Clearwater River. From there, they had continued by canoe down the Clearwater and Snake to the Columbia and, at last, safely to Astoria. Their success in coming through the dangerous wilderness had been due to the determination and experience of the band's three capable leaders, as well as to their head start, which had permitted them to get across some of the high country just ahead of the deep snows that had worn out and defeated the parties behind them.

The second crossing of the continent through what is now the United States had come to an end. In the months that followed, additional stragglers from Hunt's party reached Astoria, and others were rescued by groups sent into the interior to search for them.

Some were found sick, starving, or deranged. Others were robbed and killed by Indians before they reached the fort, or were never found.

The expedition had been a tragedy, but it had not been without its achievements. Although Hunt, the youthful businessman, had been unfit for its leadership, his bravery and persistence in forcing his way through to the Pacific had added greatly to men's knowledge of the geography and terrain of the Northwest. His ordeals on the Snake River would show future travellers where not to venture, but his route as a whole did turn out to be shorter, faster, and easier than that of Lewis and Clark; almost all portions of the trail he blazed were used thereafter by western pioneers.

As for the full Astorian venture, it fell a victim to the War of 1812 and was eventually abandoned. But it lasted long enough to help establish the claim of the United States to the lower Columbia River and the Oregon country. Back in St. Louis, where he became the operator of a large farm, postmaster of the city, and a successful dealer in furs until his death in 1842, Hunt had the satisfaction of knowing that his trials on the Snake had provided a major basis for the American claim.

Alvin Josephy, Jr., is Editor, General Books, of the American Heritage Book Division and a well-known authority on American Indians. His most recent book is The Nez Perce Indians and the Opening of the Northwest *(Yale University Press).*

The Battle Off Samar CONTINUED FROM PAGE 23

guard the exit of the San Bernardino Strait. Through that exit Kurita's still very menacing force was steadily plowing in order to turn southward off the eastern coast of Samar and come in to Leyte Gulf on October 25—its role in Sho No. 1.

Steaming at twenty knots through the narrow strait between Luzon and Samar islands, Kurita's Center Force debouched into the Philippine Sea at thirty-five minutes past midnight. In addition to the battleships *Yamato, Haruna, Kongo,* and *Nagato,* there were the heavy cruisers *Chikuma, Chokai, Haguro, Kumano, Suzuya,* and *Tone,* the smaller-gunned light cruisers *Noshiro* and *Yahagi,* and eleven destroyers.

Prepared to have to fight their way through to Leyte Gulf, the Japanese sailors were pleasantly surprised when dawn revealed nothing on the southern horizon but open water. Well beyond that horizon, below Leyte Gulf, Admiral Kinkaid's Seventh Fleet had turned southward to encounter the Japanese Southern Force under Admirals Shima and Nishimura in a triumphant fight, later to be known as the Battle of Surigao Strait. Nothing but the three light Taffy forces now stood between the U.S. invasion troops on Leyte and possible disaster. Of the three, only Taffy 3 lay directly in Kurita's path as his Center Force swept south.

This was the astonishing situation when, just after dawn on October 25, Admiral Kurita's twenty-three warships, three hours north of Leyte Gulf, ran into Admiral Clifton Sprague's small group—the 10,000-ton black-and-gray camouflaged escort carriers *Fanshaw Bay, St. Lo, White Plains, Kalinin Bay, Kitkun Bay,* and *Gambier Bay;* the 2,050-ton destroyers *Heermann, Hoel,* and *Johnston;* and the 1,275-ton destroyer escorts *Dennis, John C. Butler, Raymond,* and *Samuel B. Roberts.*

Kurita, thinking he must have stumbled onto Halsey's Third Fleet, abruptly ordered his ships into pursuit formation. Since the Center Force had been in the process of switching over from its tight night formation to a dispersed daytime deployment, the new order spread confusion through the Japanese fleet. The result was a fierce but surprisingly unco-ordinated attack on the American ships.

At 6:58 A.M., a salvo of 3,200-pound shells, each some fifty per cent heavier than the largest U.S. warship projectile, spun out of the *Yamato's* huge gun barrels. It was the first time the superbattleship had fired its 18.1-inch batteries at another ship. The *Haruna's* 14-inch guns joined in three minutes later.

At 7:01 A.M. Admiral Sprague ordered the transmission of an urgent plea for help. The request was immediately picked up, and planes from Taffies 1 and 2 were ordered to the assistance of Taffy 3. Glancing away from the enemy, Sprague noted with pride that his little fleet was following orders with the precision of a well-trained team. Straddled by the red, yellow, blue, and green splashes of marker shells, Taffy 3 was laying heavy smoke screens, the white clouds pouring from chemical generators contrasting sharply with the oily black smoke from the ships' funnels.

Launching her planes as rapidly as possible, the *White Plains* trembled violently as the mere concussion of the big enemy shells caused minor damage. Water spray from a shellburst that threw a geyser high above the carrier rained over the ship's bridge. One plane preparing to take off from the flight deck was bounced forward by the concussion of explosions pummelling the sea. Its spinning propeller bit a chunk out of the wing of another fighter. The *St. Lo,* ebony clouds pouring from her four small exhaust stacks, was also buffeted by the Japanese barrage.

Although the enemy ships had closed to within fifteen miles of their prey, they were still beyond the range of the puny U.S. 5-inch guns. If only he could keep his ships swinging in a wide circle around to the southwest without being overtaken or cut off, Sprague thought, he could hope to lead the Japanese fleet into the guns of the now-alerted battleships of the Seventh Fleet. Then, even though Kinkaid's ships were not in top shape for battle after their heavy night action in Surigao Strait against the Japanese Southern Force, the Americans would have some chance of stopping the enemy.

Deployed in a formation of two concentric circles—the six carriers forming the inner circle—the U.S. flotilla was rapidly being overtaken by the speedier enemy ships. Then, at 7:06 A.M., Taffy 3 dipped its nose into a welcome rain squall. Hindered by ineffective radar, enemy fire fell off in volume and accuracy. During the fifteen-minute respite afforded by the rain, Sprague made a decision. He would order a torpedo attack by his destroyers.

In the meantime, the first desperate strikes by the U.S. carrier planes had been made on the pursuing enemy. Dropping the small bombs and depth charges with which they had been loaded in expectation of routine missions, the Navy planes harassed the Japanese ships for twenty minutes. Bombs soon gone, they strafed with machine-gun fire. And even when their ammunition was exhausted, the pilots continued to buzz the enemy, hoping to bluff the Nipponese ships off course and give Taffy 3 a chance to escape. Only when their fuel ran low did they leave. Unable to land on their own carriers because the ships were heading downwind, the Taffy 3 planes were forced to rearm and refuel at an airstrip on the Leyte beachhead to the west, and on the flattops of Taffy 2 to the southeast. Joined by other Wildcat fighters and Avenger torpedo bombers from Taffy 2, they soon returned to the attack.

First blood for the airmen was drawn when a bomb pierced the deck of the heavy cruiser Suzuya. Shuddering under the detonation, the 14,000-ton warship slowed to twenty knots and fell behind the Japanese formation. The bold American planes, delaying the pursuers by forcing them into time-consuming evasive maneuvers, also inflicted minor damage on a few of the other Japanese ships.

The two-funnelled Johnston, which had already opened fire with her five 5-inch guns, was the first destroyer to respond to Sprague's order for a torpedo attack. As the helmsman swung the wheel hard to port, the outgunned Johnston sliced bravely through the gray sea at twenty-five knots toward the Japanese heavy cruiser Kumano. At 9,000 yards the destroyer heeled steeply over, her ten torpedoes splashing into the sea.

One of the missiles reached the sleek cruiser, blowing off its bow in a thunderous eruption of flame, smoke, and debris. Its blunted nose dipping deep into the low swells, the limping Kumano dropped astern and joined its damaged sister ship Suzuya. The battle was already over for the two badly hit cruisers.

Then luck ran out for the plucky Johnston. As she turned about, three 14-inch and three 6-inch shells slammed into her thin hull. "Like a puppy being smacked by a truck," as one of her officers put it, the ship dipped into the boiling sea and bobbed back up, her steering gear severely damaged, and many men dead and wounded both above and below decks. Commander Ernest E. Evans, who had a very short time to live, emerged from the salvo with half of his clothes blown off and minus two fingers of his left hand.

The destroyers Heerman and Hoel swept past the stricken ship toward the enemy. Although smoking and slowed to sixteen or seventeen knots, the Johnston swung awkwardly in behind the other destroyers to support them with her guns. Further back, the slower destroyer escorts formed a second attack wave. It was the story of David and Goliath in a terrifying modern context.

With guns banging and torpedoes knifing toward the Japanese ships, the Heermann and the Hoel won much-needed time for the fleeing escort carriers. But while the Heermann received reparable damage as she darted nimbly in and out of the Japanese salvos, the Hoel was less fortunate.

The first hit smashed high on the Hoel's forward superstructure, sending hot pieces of steel whistling through her radar antennas and falling on her decks. Seeking out her target through blotting rain and clouds of black and white smoke, the destroyer dashed to within 9,000 yards of the giant Kongo and released a spread of five torpedoes. Not sixty seconds later, one of the battleship's 14-inch projectiles screeched into the Hoel's side behind the funnels. Detonating in the after engine room, it hammered one of the ship's two engines into junk. A second 14-incher plowed into the ship's tail, knocking out guns, damaging the electric steering gear, and bouncing men limply off bulkheads.

Steaming on one engine and maneuvering on emergency steering apparatus, with three of her 5-inch cannons out of commission, the Hoel made another run on the enemy. The target this time was the heavy cruiser Haguro. The destroyer's five remaining torpedoes swooshed from their tubes. Then, as one of her officers later stated, the Hoel tried to "get the hell out of there." But this was easier said than done.

Barely able to keep ahead of the onrushing enemy, much less get out of the line of fire, the Hoel absorbed over forty hits as she fought back with her two remaining guns. The big battleships passing to port and the heavy cruisers steaming by to starboard deluged the quivering destroyer with heavy shells. Flames erupted from the *Hoel's* aft section, explosions shredded her superstructure, and an inferno raged inside her hull. And still the dying ship's remaining guns fired stubbornly at the thundering enemy. Then, punched full of holes, the ship finally gave up the uneven struggle. She was dead in the water, her stern almost submerged and her forward magazine ablaze, when the "abandon ship" order was given. Only a handful of the warship's crew was able to respond. At 8:55 A.M., an hour and a half after she was first hit, the *Hoel* rolled over and sank to the bottom of the Philippine Sea. Of her crew of more than 300, 253 went down with her. Fifteen of her wounded later died.

The first torpedo run was over. Despite the destruction of the *Hoel,* the skipper of the shell-peppered *Heermann* calmly radioed a modest report to Admiral Sprague: "Exercise completed."

At a quarter of eight, meanwhile, the destroyer escorts had sailed in under the cover of rain and smoke. Intended primarily for antisubmarine patrols, the lightweight escorts were no match for some of the world's most powerful ships. Yet, running to within 4,000 yards of the enemy with their 5-inch guns blazing, the American escorts managed to throw the Japanese off stride.

Dashing ahead of the pack, the little *Roberts* traded blows with the enemy heavies for forty-five minutes before she was hit. At 8:51, a heavy shell thumped into the water alongside the veering ship and plowed into her side, opening a hole below the waterline. One hit followed another, turning her into a shambles. That the heroic escort managed to go on fighting for three-quarters of an hour is an amazing tribute to her captain and crew. Answering the 14- and 8-inch shells of the Japanese cruisers with her inadequate 5-inchers, the *Roberts* was raked at point-blank range.

At approximately 9 A.M., minutes after the *Hoel* went down, two or three 14-inch shells from the *Kongo* slammed into the *Roberts'* port side. Like some gigantic can opener, the monstrous explosion tore a jagged hole over thirty feet long and seven to ten feet high in the escort's hull. The area aft of the tossing ship's funnel became what one survivor called an "inert mass of battered metal."

One gun crew, courageously ignoring flame and smoke, continued firing its weapon by hand after the ammunition hoist went out of action. Suddenly, one of the charges ignited in the hot breech before the 5-inch gun could be fired. Demolishing the cannon, the blast sent the gun crew tumbling in all directions like so many rag dolls. The first man to enter the gun mount after the shattering detonation found the gun captain, his body blown open, holding a cannon shell in his scorched hands. He was begging for help to get the fifty-four-pound projectile into the cannon. Minutes later, he was dead.

In all, the *Roberts*—the runt that fought like a champion—fired 608 shells from its 5-inch guns before the end came. She had inflicted serious damage on an enemy cruiser and had incurred almost two dozen Japanese hits. Five minutes after ten that morning, the second of the "little boys" went down off Samar. Killed in the action were 3 of her 8 officers and 86 of her 170 men.

Their torpedoes expended, the surviving escort ships fought their way back to cover the carriers. To the manmade maelstrom nature added her own effects, giving the scene an eerie quality. One moment the sun's rays would clearly illuminate the opposing forces. A few seconds later, the whole tableau would be obscured by a curtain of rain or drifting smoke. And between the clouds and the sea was the incessant lightning and thunder of gunfire. Narrowly avoiding collisions as they zigzagged to escape the enemy shells, Admiral Sprague's flotilla churned southward.

The Japanese pursuit had by now assumed a rough pattern. In an attempt to box in the carriers, which could barely reach eighteen knots, the swift Nipponese heavy cruisers raced across the wakes of the Americans to close in from the east at almost thirty knots. The Japanese destroyers and light cruisers, kept to the rear until now, pushed down along the starboard side of the baby flattops. And, at a greater distance, the *Nagato* and the huge *Yamato* were doing their best to aim straight down the back of the U.S. formation. In the meantime, the battleships *Haruna* and *Kongo* swung wide to outcruise the cruisers to the east.

For almost two and a half hours—between 6:58 and approximately 9:20—the little American carriers were under constant fire from Kurita's Center Force. Only the *Yamato* and the *Nagato,* badgered by the U.S. destroyers into performing wild, evasive maneuvers that ultimately steered them out of range, were denied the honor of remaining in the slugfest. Admiral Kurita, aboard the *Yamato,* was thus out of touch with the

This schematic drawing of the Yamato, *which confronted Taffy 3's little escort carriers off Samar, gives no clue to her huge proportions. Half again larger than the largest U.S. battleship, she displaced 68,000 tons and fired the biggest shells in naval history, each 18.1 inches in diameter.*

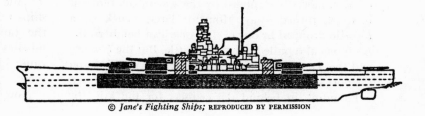

© *Jane's Fighting Ships;* REPRODUCED BY PERMISSION

action, a development that was to produce unhappy consequences for the Japanese.

As the battle unfolded, Admiral Sprague saw that the greatest immediate danger to his group were the four enemy heavy cruisers *Chikuma*, *Chokai*, *Haguro*, and *Tone*. Closer than the other Japanese ships, they were rapidly moving in from the northeast—their 8-inch shells striking into, and in many cases through, the thin-hulled carriers. Sprague told his planes and ships to concentrate on them.

Although smoke screens and maneuvering threw Japanese marksmanship off, Admiral Sprague's flagship, the *Fanshaw Bay*, received four direct hits and two near misses which killed three of her crew and wounded others. The *White Plains*, the *Kitkun Bay*, and the *St. Lo* got off lightly; but the *Kalinin Bay* took more than a dozen heavy projectiles, miraculously remaining afloat.

Shrewd guesswork and clever steering by her skipper saved the *Gambier Bay*, steaming on the exposed left rear corner of the U.S. formation, for a full twenty-five minutes. Then, at 8:10 A.M., a shell from a Japanese cruiser hit the aft end of the carrier's flight deck. Fire broke out in the ship's hangar as the projectile sheared through the upper deck. More heavy-caliber shots slashed in. A gaping hole was torn in the *Gambier Bay*'s forward port engine room, flooding it with cascading water. Less than half an hour after first being struck, the escort carrier slowed to eleven knots and dropped back. The heavy cruisers *Chikuma*, *Chokai*, and *Haguro*, the light cruiser *Noshiro*, and a Nipponese destroyer poured salvo after salvo into the blazing carrier's hull. Steering and power aboard the *Gambier Bay* were shot out, the after engine room was flooded, and men cursed and died at their posts. Efforts by the destroyers *Johnston* and *Heermann* to draw attention away from the dying CVE failed.

By 8:45 A.M., the carrier was entirely without headway and was settling. Five minutes later, the 750 living of the *Gambier Bay*'s 854-man crew began going over the side. Still the enemy shells came, killing some men in the water. Seven minutes after 9 A.M., their ship turned turtle and sank. Fighting the suction of the plunging 10,000-ton flattop, the survivors struggled to keep afloat until help came. It would come—almost forty hours later.

Meanwhile Taffy 3 aircraft pounced like hawks on the enemy cruisers. Bomb bursts erupted on the ships as the Japanese paid for their lack of air power. The *Chokai*, mortally wounded by the sea-and-air blows it received, turned away. Moments later, struck by a torpedo dropped by one of the American bombers, the *Chikuma* also pulled out of the battle. But the *Haguro* and the *Tone*, the remaining enemy heavy cruisers on the port side of the American formation, pressed closer.

Pounding in behind the cruisers for the kill, the

"WHERE IS THE JAP FLEET—NOW?"

In the days after Pearl Harbor, incredulous Americans often asked, "Where is the United States fleet?" The news of the great naval victory in the Philippines evoked a triumphant counterquestion in this typical American newspaper cartoon.

closest of the Japanese battleships—the *Haruna*—suddenly veered to the southeast. The big ship's observers could see, about twenty miles away, the northernmost ships of Admiral Felix B. Stump's Taffy 2. With the Imperial Navy's penchant for dividing its forces, the *Haruna* swung her heavy two-gun turrets toward the new target. Although the 29,300-ton leviathan lobbed 14-inch shells at the Taffy 2 ships for almost half an hour, it failed to score a hit.

Nipponese destroyers were now also closing in on Taffy 3. Led by the light cruiser *Yahagi*, four of them streaked in from the west for a torpedo attack on the crippled *Johnston*. Her decks littered with wreckage tinted by blood and the dye of enemy marker shells, the *Johnston* challenged the Japanese attack with her two operational guns. Trading blows with five undamaged ships, the limping destroyer scored a number of hits on the 6,000-ton *Yahagi*. A U.S. plane joined the fray with chattering 50-caliber machine guns. Twenty minutes after starting their attack, the enemy ships released their torpedoes and turned about. But the Japanese had been tricked into releasing their missiles prematurely. Losing their aim and speed because of the extreme range, the torpedoes failed to score.

Now the cruisers *Haguro* and *Tone* swept by on the

opposite side of the *Johnston*. The American destroyer rolled under the rain of shells for another thirty minutes. Fires raged through the beaten ship, cremating the wounded and dead huddled in the wreckage, trapping the living in the steel coffin of her hull. Her ammunition blew up in a series of blasts, adding to the carnage. Her engines gone, her communication system obliterated, the wallowing destroyer still barked pugnaciously at the enemy with her remaining cannon. Then, at 9:45 A.M., Commander Evans ordered the surviving crewmen off the doomed ship.

Like Indians in a western movie, the Japanese destroyers steamed around the settling *Johnston* in a circle until the riddled vessel turned over and sank at 10:10 A.M.

The survivors in the water watched their blazing ship disappear. One of them reported that as it went down a Japanese destroyer captain saluted. Most, swimming or clinging to life rafts and debris, were numbed and shocked. One moment they had been going about their daily routine; the next they were racing to their battle stations. And then, after hours of brain-pounding battle that demanded automatic response, they had been cast into a tropical sea shadowed by the haze of gunsmoke and burning ships. There was now only the slapping of waves and the gasping of hoarse voices. A torpedoman, with a casualness produced by shock, remarked to a fellow survivor that they'd gotten off all torpedoes.

In a sea alive with activity, the fate of the *Johnston's* crew was to be a harsh one. Only 141 of her crew of 327 would be saved—49 were killed during the action, 45 died of their wounds after abandoning ship, and 92 (including Commander Evans) perished while awaiting rescue. Sharks got at least one man; the others succumbed to exposure.

As the battle raged, the ultimate weaknesses of the Japanese attack finally made themselves felt. Hampered by a combination of rain squalls, smoke screens, stubborn American resistance, poor communications, lack of co-ordination, and, above all, the lack of air strength, the enemy attack fell apart. The *Yamato* and the *Nagato* had let themselves wander off; the *Haruna* was in pursuit of Taffy 2.

Expecting at any moment to be swimming for his life, Clifton Sprague had been grimly sizing up the situation as the enemy salvos boomed into the midst of Taffy 3. His ships had arced into their southwesterly course as ordered. Ahead and a bit to the right he could make out the dark outline of Samar some thirty miles away. Then, at 9:25, as he concentrated on evading the torpedoes launched minutes before by the *Yahagi* and her destroyers, the skipper of Taffy 3 was treated to the sweetest words he could ever hope to hear.

"Goddamit, boys, they're getting away!" called out

a signalman on the bridge of the *Fanshaw Bay*.

Unable to keep in touch with his fleet because of bad radio communication, Admiral Kurita had launched the *Yamato's* two reconnaissance planes less than an hour apart to survey the situation. Both were shot down some fifteen minutes after they were catapulted from the stern of the battleship. Unaware that his ships were finally closing in on their prey—with victory off Samar still possible—the confused Japanese admiral had decided to regroup his fleet before a fuel shortage and the relentless American air attacks put it out of action. At 9:11 A.M. Kurita had ordered all his units to take a northerly course.

Despite the blows dealt to Kurita's ships, there was precious little to keep his fleet from blasting its way through Taffy 3 to Leyte Gulf. Far to the north, off Cape Engaño, too distant to do any good, Halsey's Third Fleet was only now reluctantly giving up its chase of Ozawa's Northern Force and turning about in answer to urgent messages from Admiral Kinkaid and Pacific Fleet Headquarters at Pearl Harbor. To the south, Kinkaid's Seventh Fleet was on the other side of Leyte Gulf. Its ships, low on fuel and ammunition, were still busy with mopping up what remained of the Japanese southern thrust.

Yet it takes no great stretch of the imagination to understand the indecision and uncertainty that marked Takeo Kurita's actions at this point in the battle. He had been forced to swim for his life when the *Atago* was sunk on the twenty-third. The Center Force had been under repeated air assault since it first entered the Sibuyan Sea. He had received no news of Ozawa's success in decoying Halsey, and was still under the impression that Taffy 3 was part of the U.S. Third Fleet. Discouraged by reports of the Surigao Strait action, he felt his ships were alone. Fatigued, his nerves strained, Kurita decided to disregard the order that called for his charging into Leyte Gulf. Instead, as a face-saving gesture, the Center Force would shift to a new target.

Earlier in the day, an American task force had been reported in the Philippine Sea to the northeast. Kurita would attack it. Several hours spent in search of the phantom U.S. force proved fruitless. Assisted in his decision by the nagging persuasion of U.S. Navy planes that continued to peck at his ships, the Center Force commander finally called off the hunt and ordered his fleet to head back where it came from.

Suffering the final indignity of being mistakenly attacked by two Japanese land-based aircraft, the Center Force slipped westward through San Bernardino Strait a few hours later. Fast warships from Halsey's Third Fleet reached the strait soon afterward, too late to catch Kurita but in time to bag one lagging Japanese destroyer.

But despite Kurita's departure, the ordeal of Taffy 3 was not quite over.

At 10:50 A.M., soon after Admiral Sprague ordered Taffy 3's pilots to return to their carriers, five Japanese planes had roared in just over the wave-tops. Soaring upward, they climbed a mile above the carriers and suddenly dived down. The Divine Wind—the newly organized Kamikaze suicide corps—was about to wreak its vengeance on Taffy 3.

A single-engined Zero fighter crashed on the port side of the *Kitkun Bay* and bounced into the sea. Its bomb, however, exploded and damaged the carrier. Tensely watching from the *Fanshaw Bay*, Clifton Sprague saw the ship's 40- and 20-millimeter anti-aircraft fire chew apart two of the diving suicide planes. They fell into the ocean. The *White Plains* sent streams of tracer bullets into the remaining Kamikazes. One of the enemy exploded a few yards behind the flattop, injuring eleven Americans and spraying the deck with debris and pieces of the pilot. The other plane, its engine sputtering, swerved toward the *St. Lo*. With a grinding of metal and a shower of sparks, the Zero tore into the carrier. A ball of fire sent clouds of smoke boiling heavenward. One explosion followed the other as bombs and torpedoes stored inside the *St. Lo* were set off. Torn apart and burning from stem to stern, the little ship that had survived the *Yamato*'s great shells sank in less than twenty minutes. She was the first major victim of the Divine Wind. Of her more than 800 men, 754 were saved by Taffy 3.

There was more to come. At 11:10 A.M. Admiral Sprague's little fleet was attacked by enemy torpedo planes. Two were immediately shot down by U.S. interceptors near the *Kitkun Bay*. A third exploded almost on top of the carrier and showered the ship with flaming aircraft parts. The *Kalinin Bay* was severely damaged by planes making suicide runs. One smashed into her flight deck, the other caught her on the starboard side in the after exhaust pipe. Only the *Fanshaw Bay* escaped unscathed.

By 11:30 A.M. the attacks had ended. Admiral Sprague's battered flotilla headed into Leyte Gulf for a much-needed rest. In an over-all battle where American naval forces far outnumbered the Japanese, Taffy 3 had been overwhelmed by almost 2-to-1 odds and immeasurably greater fire power—yet Clifton Sprague and his men had made a fighting retreat and convinced Admiral Kurita that he was engaged with a full-fledged fleet.

Having dispatched the surviving Taffy 3 escort ships to pick up crewmen of the stricken *St. Lo*, Admiral Sprague asked Seventh Fleet Headquarters to handle the rescue of the survivors of the *Gambier Bay*, *Johnston*, *Roberts*, and *Hoel*. Unfortunately, poor co-ordination, a sudden flurry of Japanese suicide plane attacks, and erroneous position reports radioed in by aircraft delayed these rescue operations for almost two days.

Finally, at 10:29 on the night of October 26, a seven-ship detail personally ordered out by Admiral Kinkaid obtained results. Guided by flares fired high above the rough black sea, the vessels under Lieutenant Commander J. A. Baxter picked up more than 700 survivors from the *Gambier Bay*. Suffering from exposure, hunger, and fatigue, the carrier survivors had clung to life rafts for some thirty-nine hours and drifted almost to the coast of Samar before being sighted. Many had drowned. With the coming of dawn, survivors from the *Johnston*, *Roberts*, and *Hoel* were found.

The last raft, containing fifteen men from the *Johnston*, was spotted at 9:30 A.M. on the twenty-seventh—forty-eight hours after the sinking of the destroyer. By early the following morning, the 1,150 survivors of the Taffy 3 ships sunk by the Center Force had been transferred from Baxter's seven vessels to hospital ships and transports in Leyte Gulf.

The over-all Battle for Leyte Gulf, spread across a total area twice the size of Texas, was the greatest sea fight in history. Every element of naval warfare, from submarine to aircraft, was involved. And when it was over, the Imperial Japanese Navy had ceased to exist as a fighting unit. The United States and her allies had undisputed control of the Pacific Ocean.

Between October 23 and 26, Japan's Sho Plan No. 1 cost her three battleships, four carriers, ten cruisers, and almost a dozen other fighting ships. Scores of aircraft and some 10,000 Japanese seamen were also lost by the Empire. The U.S. losses added up to 2,800 lives, about two hundred aircraft, and six warships. Taffy 3, bearing the brunt of the punishment, had lost the escort carriers *Gambier Bay* and *St. Lo*, the destroyers *Johnston* and *Hoel*, the destroyer escort *Samuel B. Roberts*, 128 planes, and 1,583 men killed and missing.

"In no engagement of its entire history," Samuel Eliot Morison has written, "has the United States Navy shown more gallantry, guts and gumption than in those two morning hours between 0730 and 0930 off Samar."

Rear Admiral Clifton Sprague had his own observation on the battle: "The failure of the enemy . . . to completely wipe out all vessels of this task unit can be attributed to our successful smoke screen, our torpedo counterattack, continuous harassment of enemy by bomb, torpedo and strafing air attacks, timely maneuvers, and the definite partiality of Almighty God."

Mr. Deac, public information specialist and speech writer for the Air Force Eastern Test Range at Cape Kennedy, has been a newspaper editor, advertising copywriter, public-relations administrator, and government historian.

Rebel in a Wing Collar CONTINUED FROM PAGE 29

before the public," the Baltimore *Herald* reported:

There were 500 in line. Mrs. Annie L. Diggs, the Populist agitator of Kansas [was first] . . . then Coxey's seventeen-year-old daughter in white on a cream-colored steed, representing the goddess of peace; Carl Browne on a great gray Percheron stallion; General Jacob Sechler Coxey, his wife, and infant son . . . together in another carriage; Virginia La Valette, said to be an actress, on horseback, draped in an American flag as the Philadelphia Commune's goddess of peace; [then] the unemployed carrying white flags of peace on staves and the nondescript banners setting forth the doctrines of reincarnation, good roads, and enmity to plutocrats sprinkled through the caravan.

Arriving at the east steps of the Capitol, Coxey attempted to address the crowd, but was told it was against the law. He then asked permission to read a written protest, which was also denied him. At this point, just as he handed a written copy of the protest to the press, the crowd became unruly and what was described as a riot broke out. Browne's horse leaped a low wall, followed by an entire squadron of mounted policemen. Less than five minutes later, order was restored, and Coxey, Browne, and Christopher Columbus Jones were placed under arrest. On May 8, the three were found guilty of walking on the grass of the Capitol, fined five dollars each, and sentenced to twenty days in jail. Meanwhile, all across the nation, scattered bits of the army continued to march toward Washington, unaware that the cause was already lost. About a hundred or more from the main army camped briefly across the Maryland line, but after many complaints by farmers of food being stolen, the governor sent a number of Baltimore policemen to round up the men, about eighty of whom were jailed as vagrants.

So ended what some had called the "red menace" of 1894. Carl Browne continued to agitate for organized labor until his death in 1913. Coxey returned to Ohio, but did not sink into the oblivion that would surely have come to him if he had been no more than a publicity-seeker. Indeed, for another half-century, he made further attempts to win over Congress, and in 1914 led a second, sadly unnoticed march on Washington, again for public-works projects. A lesser spirit might have quit then, but Coxey was a man who shrugged off abuse, derision, and failure. It did not impair his sense of his own immortal fame to be named candidate for President in 1932 on the Farmer-Labor ticket (in Minnesota, he received 5,371 votes, almost as many as the Communist candidate), and to lose.

His struggles were not altogether unrewarded. In the 1930's he had the satisfaction of seeing some of his ideas incorporated in Franklin D. Roosevelt's public-works projects: he had been, in his time, a kind of harbinger of the New Deal.

His final ambition, to be a centenarian, was denied him: he died in 1951, at the age of ninety-seven. Several children survived him, but not that infant son he had carried down Pennsylvania Avenue in 1894, Legal Tender Coxey by name.

George Gipe is the documentary editor for WMAR-TV in Baltimore. He has been a Fulbright scholar, a free-lance writer, and a producer of numerous documentary programs for television.

For further reading: Coxey's Army, *by Donald L. McMurry (Little, Brown, 1929);* Baker's Dozen, *by Russel B. Nye (Michigan State, 1956);* Dreamers of the American Dream, *by Stewart H. Holbrook (Doubleday, 1957).*

The Boston Massacre

CONTINUED FROM PAGE 10

stood the prisoners and their uneasy lawyers. Ironically, after the frantic search for defense attorneys, the Crown had almost as much trouble finding men willing to serve on the prosecution side. Jonathan Sewall, the colony's attorney general, handed up the indictment and disappeared from Boston, declaring that he would never appear in another court in that town. This may have been in part a maneuver to delay the trial. In the weeks succeeding the Massacre, Boston's inflamed state of mind made the possibility of an objective jury almost laughable.

But Samuel Adams was not to be easily put off. On the thirteenth of March, a town meeting resolved "That the selectmen be desired to employ one or more counsel to offer to the King's attorney as assistants to him in the trial of the murtherers now committed; and in case the King's attorney should refuse such assistance and the relatives of those persons who were murthered should apply for it, that then the town will bear the expense that may accrue thereby." The court soon appointed Samuel Quincy, Josiah Quincy's elder brother and a convinced Tory, to head the prosecution. Assisting him as the town's designee was attorney Robert Treat Paine, a staunch Liberty man.

On March 14, the day after the term opened, two of the judges declared themselves ill and announced a determination to adjourn to the second Tuesday in June. A committee of Liberty men swiftly appeared in court, with Samuel Adams and John Hancock as their spokesmen. In his quavering voice, gesturing with his palsied hands, Adams made what one observer called "a *very pathetic* [emotional] speech," calling on the court to proceed to the trial without delay. Governor Hutchinson described Adams as followed by "a vast concourse of people." The terrified judges, Hutchinson reported, "altered their determination and resolved to go on with the business. This, they assured me, was contrary to their inclination but they were under duress and afraid to offend the town."

A tax stamp

Captain Thomas Preston, meanwhile, tried to launch a small propaganda campaign on his own behalf. An Anglo-Irishman, forty years old with fifteen years of army service on his record, he was, compared to the other British soldiers in the garrison, well liked by the people of Boston. Various letters describe him as "amiable" and as being "a benevolent, humane man." Hoping no doubt to enlarge this image, he had the following "card" published in the Boston *Gazette*.

Messieurs Edes and Gill, permit me thro' the channel of your Paper, to return my Thanks in the most publick Manner to the Inhabitants in general of this Town—who throwing aside all *Party* and Prejudice, have with the utmost Humanity and Freedom stept forth Advocates for Truth in Defence of my injured Innocence, in the late unhappy Affair that happened on Monday Night last: and to assure them, that I shall ever have the highest Sense of the *Justice* they have done me, which will be ever gratefully remembered, by Their most obliged and most obedient humble Servant, Thomas Preston.

In New York, this gesture struck General Gage as the height of folly. "I can't be a proper judge at this distance," he wrote to Colonel Dalrymple, "but I wish he may not have been too premature in that measure; and if a legal proceedings are hereafter made use of against him, they will justify themselves by his own words."

Through late March and April, Samuel Adams kept his town meeting in almost continuous session by endlessly delaying matters of business. This gave him a perfectly legal device to maintain a relentless pressure on Governor Hutchinson and the judges.

The beleaguered Hutchinson decided that he would have to offer his enemies a sacrifice to allay their ferocity. Two weeks before the Massacre, a Custom House employee, Ebenezer Richardson, had gotten into a brawl with some boys who chased him home with a barrage of icy snowballs, stones, and brickbats. They continued the bombardment on his house, smashing most of the windows. The enraged Tory suddenly thrust a musket loaded with birdshot from an upstairs window. "By God," he shouted, "I'll make a lane through you." The gun boomed and most of the charge struck a twelve-year-old boy, who died that night. For Samuel Adams, Richardson was, of course, a very small fish. But his case did, in sequence of time, come first. Adams was therefore helpless to object when the judges moved to put Richardson in the dock.

Richardson had even more trouble procuring legal aid than Preston and his soldiers. Not a single attorney volunteered, and when the court appointed Samuel Fitch, he agreed to serve under violent protestations of duress, then became conveniently ill when the case went to trial. The court then appointed Josiah Quincy, Jr., an equally reluctant if more idealistic advocate. Only recently have we learned that the man who directed Richardson's defense was John Adams. The notes and documents pertaining to the case were discovered in John's legal files by the editors of the Adams Papers. With Samuel Quincy and Robert Treat Paine handling the prosecution, Richardson's case became almost a rehearsal for the Massacre trial.

"A vast concourse of rabble," as one Tory described his fellow Bostonians, packed the courtroom. They growled their disapproval when the three judges unanimously agreed that from the testimony of witnesses on both sides, the charge against Richardson could amount to no more than manslaughter. Justice Peter Oliver went even further and declared to the jury that in his opinion the case was justifiable homicide. Whereupon an improper Bostonian shouted from the crowd: "Damn that judge. If I was nigh him I would give it to him." When Oliver finished speaking, someone in the crowd roared out: "Remember, Jury, you are on oath. Blood requires blood."

The jury found Richardson guilty of first-degree murder, and only vigorous exertion by the sheriff and town constables prevented the mob from taking him outside and hanging him on the spot.

The judges, aghast at the jury's complete disregard of their charge, refused to sentence Richardson. He was remanded to jail, where he was to languish for another two years. His case, however, made it look certain that trying Preston and the soldiers right away would result in their conviction. "Procrastination is our only course as things are now situated," wrote Colonel Dalrymple to General Gage.

Samuel Adams and his friends continued to agitate for instant justice. Once more they appeared in the courtroom and harangued the judges, threatening to withhold their salaries if they delayed any longer. But Hutchinson, who had the courage of his convictions, finally won the seesaw battle. Under his direction, the court constantly met and adjourned, met and adjourned. Then Hutchinson shifted the next meeting of the judiciary to Cambridge, proclaiming it a necessity to avoid the threats of the Boston mob. This inspired (on June 1, 1770) what Hutchinson ironically called "a jovial celebration . . . at Boston in opposition to me," which involved roasting an ox whole on the Common and a great dinner at Faneuil Hall. While toasts were being drunk to liberty, the judges quietly adjourned the court *sine die* (without setting a day to reconvene), automatically continuing to the next term the question of the soldiers' fate. Hutchinson wrote proudly to Gage, describing how he had "procured without any tumult a continuance of the trial to the next term."

Through the hot Boston summer Preston and his men sat in their cells. Preston's fortunes, which seemed for a while to be rising, took a sharp downward turn when a Tory version of the Massacre, first published in England, appeared in the Boston *Gazette*. The Captain was soon writing Gage that he feared the mob

was planning an attack on the jail to murder him and his men in their cells. Though Hutchinson doubted that the Liberty people would make such an attack before the trial, he recommended to Sheriff Steven Greenleaf that he take the keys from the jailkeeper at night, just in case.

Meanwhile, Hutchinson was having his troubles with the judges. Twice during the summer, Chief Justice Benjamin Lynde, who was over seventy, came to him with his resignation. Justice Edmund Trowbridge was at least as terrified. Only Judge Peter Oliver stood firm, ignoring personal threats in the newspapers. Another worry was the lack of enthusiasm which the Tories anticipated in the soldiers' attorneys. Loyalist Auchmuty bluntly told Hutchinson he did not think Preston had a chance.

Nevertheless, early in September, with Hutchinson's approval, Preston began to press for a trial. Actually Hutchinson was still certain Preston would be found guilty, but he wanted the matter settled early in the fall, with sentencing delayed until the opening of the March term. This might give him time to get a ship to England and back with a King's pardon to save Preston's neck.

The justices, however, reserved their own opinion of when they should risk their lives by bringing Preston to trial: they went on circuit into the country. First, however, they did bring the Captain and his eight soldiers into the courtroom for arraignment. Each pleaded "Not guilty," and "for trial put himself upon God and the country."

At this point John Adams played a surprise card, one he had been holding very close to his vest. He made a motion to try Captain Preston and the soldiers separately. The court granted it. The soldiers immediately decided they were to be the sacrificial lambs, and forwarded a plaintive petition to the court: "May it please Your Honors, we poor distressed prisoners beg that ye would be so good as to lett us have our trial at the same

The landing of British troops to garrison Boston in 1768 profoundly irritated most of the natives.

time with our Captain, for we did our Captain's orders and if we don't obey his command we should have been confined and shott for not doing it. . . ." This only confirmed defense fears that Preston and his men would each accuse the other if tried jointly, and in the confusion the jury would decide to hang them all. But as we shall soon see, this was not the only reason for Adams' unexpected motion.

Not until October 24, 1770, did the judges return and the lawyers assemble to impanel a jury to decide Captain Preston's fate. Almost immediately it became evident that the court and all the lawyers were involved in a curious kind of collusion. Adams, the acknowledged leader of the defense, challenged every juror who came from within the city limits of Boston, quickly rejecting the eighteen men who had been selected by the Boston town meeting of August 24, 1770. When the legally summoned jurors were used up, it was the custom of the day to allow the sheriff to contribute "talesmen." By no coincidence, every talesman produced by the sheriff for Preston's trial came from outside Boston. Indeed, a study of the jury list reveals that five of the twelve selected were later Loyalist exiles.

These maneuvers must have been obvious to Samuel Adams. They were beyond all doubt known to John Adams and Josiah Quincy. Why did Samuel Adams by silence and inaction give tacit approval? A nod from him, and his well-disciplined bullyboys could have filled the courtroom as they did at Richardson's trial

A failure in business, Sam Adams became one of the most successful politicians in American history. From 1764 until 1776 he bent all of his talents toward contesting British sovereignty.

and terrified the judges and jurors into submission. But there is no evidence of any disorder during Preston's trial, nor at the trial of the soldiers. The change of tactics is startling, and there is nothing in the written evidence of the Massacre story that explains it.

The answer must lie in the political struggle that surrounded the trials. By this time, John Adams and Josiah Quincy had, thanks to a liberal supply of sovereigns from General Gage, obtained depositions from dozens of people who had been witnesses to various aspects of the bloody deed. These statements conflicted so totally with the evidence advanced by the Liberty men in their ninety-six depositions that there was only one possible conclusion—someone was committing perjury. Worse, the evidence advanced by the witnesses Adams and Quincy uncovered put the town of Boston in a most unholy light. For the first time the Loyalists had a weapon with which they could smite Samuel Adams hard. But Sam on his side retained the weapon he knew and handled best: the Boston mob.

Even with the packed jury, Preston's case was by no means a sure thing. The prosecution attacked vigorously, parading witness after witness to the stand for the better part of two days; all of them agreed that the Captain gave the order to fire—and, equally important, that there was no provocation for it beyond name-calling and a few snowballs from the crowd gathered in King Street.

The defense attorneys did little to dispute these assertions in their cross-examination. But they did shake the believability of many witnesses by pointing out strange confusions in their testimony. Some swore the Captain stood in front of the men; others said he stood behind them. Several said that the Captain had on a "cloth color" surtout (a kind of overcoat); almost as many said they distinctly saw him in his bright red regimentals.

After a prosecution summation by Samuel Quincy, in which he accused Preston of "murder with malice aforethought," the defense produced their witnesses. The first few disputed the prosecution's claim that the crowd was small and peaceful, but said nothing that would stir an already tired jury. (It was the first time in Massachusetts' memory that a murder trial had lasted more than a day.) Then John Adams produced a merchant named Richard Palmes, and the courtroom came to life. Mr. Palmes was the real reason for the separate trials. He had earlier given a lengthy deposition supposedly supporting the Liberty side of the story. Even a cursory reading of this told a lawyer as keen as John Adams that detaching Preston from his men converted Palmes into a witness for the Captain.

Palmes knew it, and had desperately tried to decamp from Boston. John Adams had kept him in town by court order. On the stand, the reluctant Palmes was forced to repeat his sworn deposition. He told of stepping up to Preston as he joined his soldiers and asking: "Sir, I hope you don't intend the soldiers shall fire on the inhabitants."

"He said, 'by no means.' The instant he spoke I saw something resembling snow or ice strike the grenadier on the Captain's right hand, being the only one then at his right. [The grenadier] instantly stepped one foot back and fired the first gun. . . . The gun scorched the nap of my surtout at the elbow."

Other witnesses substantiated Palmes' statement. As a good lawyer, Adams also brought in a few people who bolstered the self-defense side of Preston's plea. But in his summation, he made it clear that Palmes was his key witness. Coolly, he noted that the mortified merchant was "an inhabitant of the town and therefore not prejudiced in favor of the soldiers." Robert Auchmuty, summing up after Adams, declared that Palmes' evidence "may be opposed to all the Crown's evidence." He went on to give an impressive speech, citing a wealth of precedents in the common law which permitted soldiers or other persons to kill rioters or even individuals who attacked them and threatened them with serious injury. Auchmuty's knowledge of the law was considered weak, but he sounded formidable as he cited case after case from Coke and other great authorities on English law. Undoubtedly he was using John Adams' research. But he put it together with an enthusiasm and flair that surprised and delighted Preston and the Tories who had been doubting him. His performance can probably be explained by a letter General Gage wrote to Colonel Dalrymple, "I am sorry," the British commander in chief said, "you doubt Mr. Auchmuty's zeal or good intentions. . . . If you find it necessary, you should encourage him, for very particular reports are to be made of every circumstance of the tryal." Caught between the threat of royal censure and his dread of the Boston mob, Auchmuty followed his Loyalist leanings and performed brilliantly.

Robert Treat Paine valiantly tried to rescue the prosecution's case. But he could not explain away Palmes. He called him "their principal witness" and admitted he was "a gentleman who I can by no means suppose would be guilty of a known falsehood." Paine could only maintain that this staunch Son of Liberty was "certainly mistaken," and fumble to an emotional peroration, calling on the jury to "find such a verdict as the laws of God, of nature and your own conscience will ever approve."

Now came the judges' charges to the jury. There were four sitting—Chief Justice Lynde and Justices John Cushing, Peter Oliver, and Edmund Trowbridge. Trowbridge was considered the best legal mind in

Thomas Hutchinson, lieutenant governor of Massachusetts at the time of the Massacre trial, was a thoroughbred New Englander, but also an arch-royalist who hated the idea of rebellion.

Massachusetts. Stately in their white wigs and long red (for a murder trial) robes, they proceeded to examine the evidence and the law. Trowbridge spoke first, pointing out the contradictory accounts given by the witnesses and declaring that it did not appear to him that the prisoner gave orders to fire. But even if the jury should think otherwise, they surely could not call his crime murder. The people assembled were "a riotous mob" who had murderously attacked the prisoner and his party. If Preston was guilty of any offense, it could only be excusable homicide. The other three judges concurred. Oliver added, "in a very nervous and pathetic manner," that he was resolved to do his duty to his God, his King, and his country, and despise both insults and threats.

The jury was then locked up for the night. Within three hours they voted to acquit Preston and so reported it to the assembled court the next morning. The Captain was immediately released from jail and rushed by boat to Castle William, where the guns of his regiment guaranteed his safety against possible revenge from the Boston mob. But Samuel Adams' obvious acquiescence in the choice of a packed jury made it clear that he had long since agreed to let Captain Preston go in peace. His men were another matter.

Thus far, John Adams, with Josiah Quincy's help, had maintained his perilous balancing act. At one point during the five days of Preston's trial, he had objected angrily when Auchmuty tried to advance more evidence of a Liberty conspiracy to incite a riot.

The Tories on the bench had stressed mob violence in their remarks to the jury; yet the violent side of the evidence had played only a minor role in Preston's trial. It had to be the heart of the soldiers' case. That they had fired their guns was beyond debating; five men were dead to prove it.

There was another hint of the way the local wind was blowing: Auchmuty now withdrew from the soldiers' defense, and another attorney, Sampson Salter Blowers, was appointed in his place. Like Quincy, he was young and comparatively inexperienced. Thus almost full responsibility for the soldiers' fate, both in a public and a private sense, fell on the stocky shoulders of John Adams.

If he had any illusions about the tactics of the opposition, they vanished when he picked up the Boston *Gazette* on the Monday before the trial began. "Is it then a dream—murder on the 5th of March with the dogs greedily licking human blood in King Street? Some say that righteous heaven will avenge it. And what says the Law of God? *Whoso sheddeth Man's Blood, by Man shall his Blood be shed!*" And the *Gazette* quoted at length from a sermon preached by the Reverend Doctor Chauncy, senior minister of Boston, declaring that should the soldiers be convicted of murder, Governor Hutchinson would never dare grant them a reprieve: "Surely he would not suffer the town and land to lie under the defilement of blood! Surely he would not make himself a partaker in the guilt of murder by putting a stop to the shedding of their blood, who have murderously spilt the blood of others."

On the day the second trial began, the audience was a good barometer of the local atmosphere. At Preston's trial the benches had been filled by Tories and army officers. Now the courtroom was jammed to the windows with townspeople. Shorthand-writer John Hodgson, who recorded the trial, complained that he did not have room to move his elbow. Outside, snow was falling, and the bailiffs had to light candles against the gloom. People shivered in winter clothes; the two small stoves in the room seemed to have no effect whatsoever on the pervading chill.

The prisoners were brought to the bar. Their blazing red coats set off their faces, drawn and pale from almost nine months in jail. The clerk of the court read an enlarged indictment to them. It accused them of murdering, besides Crispus Attucks, Samuel Maverick, a seventeen-year-old apprentice boy; Samuel Gray, a former employee of (but no relation to) the owner of Gray's rope works; James Caldwell, a sailor from a Massachusetts coasting vessel; and one Patrick Carr, known as "the Irish teague."

The jury was now chosen, and Adams and Quincy challenged and rejected no less than thirty prospects, forcing the sheriff to summon eight talesmen. As in Preston's case, the accepted jurymen were all from neighboring towns—Roxbury, Dedham, Milton, Hingham—and one, Isaiah Thayer, was from Adams' home town of Braintree. But there is no evidence that any had Tory leanings.

The prosecution opened with a brief, low-keyed talk by Samuel Quincy. He declared that the trial involved the "most melancholy event that has yet taken place on the continent of America, and perhaps of the greatest expectation of any that has yet come before a tribunal of civil justice in this part of the British dominions." He vowed to make no appeal to partiality or prejudice but to conduct himself "with decency and candor," with one object—"simply that of truth."

Whereupon he began summoning witnesses by the dozen. The first several (one was Jonathan W. Austin, John Adams' clerk) simply identified various soldiers and reported seeing one or two of the victims fall. Things heated up when Edward Langford, a town watchman, took the stand. He testified that Samuel Gray was standing beside him in the front rank of the crowd in the most peaceable manner, without any weapon, not even a snowball: "His hands were in his bosom." According to Langford, Gray asked him what was going on. Langford replied he did not know, and almost immediately Matthew Killroy's gun went off and Samuel Gray fell, striking Langford's left foot. A parade of succeeding witnesses repeatedly identified Killroy as Gray's assassin.

Richard Palmes returned to testify, for the prosecution this time, and was obviously much more comfortable about it. He identified bald-headed Hugh Montgomery, one of the sentries, and testified that he had knocked Montgomery down—but only *after* the grenadier had fired his gun, and was attempting to run Palmes through with his bayonet.

Subsequent testimony, notably by Nicholas Ferreter, supplied interesting background information for the "massacre." Ferreter was a worker at Gray's rope works. He reported that on Friday, March 2, during the lunch hour at Gray's, Samuel Gray hailed a passing soldier and asked him if he wanted work. "Yes," said the poorly paid redcoat, "I do, faith." Well, said Gray in pure Anglo-Saxon, he could go clean his outhouse. The soldier's temper exploded. He took a swing at Gray, and other ropemakers rushed to Gray's assistance. Ferreter described how he "knocked up his [the soldier's] heels, his coat flew open and out dropped a naked cutlass which I took up and carried off with me." The soldier was soon back with a dozen of his fellows, among them Matthew Killroy. A battle royal

On the Death of Five young Men who was Murthered, *March* 5th 1770. By the 29th Regiment.

Macabre coffin lids showing the victims' initials decorated the title page of this broadside published by Paul Revere.

ensued, until the ropewalk owner, John Gray, stopped it. That afternoon the soldiers returned in force, and this time the rope workers, in a furious brawl, drove them back to their barracks.

Ill feeling on the part of the British garrison toward the populace was thus well established. Another point in the prosecution's attack was the conduct of the soldiers on the night of the killing. There was, they argued, a plot afoot among the members of the 29th Regiment to attack anyone they caught on the street. Nathaniel Appleton told how a dozen soldiers with drawn bayonets had attacked him on the steps of his house and only fast footwork got him inside in time to bolt the door. John Appleton, "a young lad," told how he had been with his nine-year-old brother in King Street when twenty soldiers with cutlasses in their hands attacked him. He begged them to spare his life, he testified, and one said, "No, damn you, we will kill you all," and struck at his head with a sheathed cutlass. Thomas Marshall told how he saw "a party from the main guard, ten or twelve, come rushing out violently. I saw their arms glitter by the moonlight, hallooing, 'Damn them, where are they, by Jesus, let them come.'"

Finally, to certify the hideous and bloodthirsty character of the defendants, one Joseph Crosswell testified that the next morning he saw blood dried on five or six inches of Killroy's bayonet.

Samuel Quincy summed up the prosecution's evidence. He dwelt at length on testimony that accused Killroy of firing directly at Gray, and deduced that the private was guilty of murder with malice. He then deplored the conduct of the soldiers before the riot, maintaining that the church bells had rung because it was the soldiers who, rushing to the street, had cried the word "fire." "It is probable," declared Quincy darkly, "the word fire was the watchword. It appears to me that if we can believe the evidence, they had a design of attacking and slaughtering the inhabitants that night and they could have devised no better method to draw out the inhabitants unarmed than to cry fire!" Finally, he hammered again at Killroy, reminding the jury that it is "immaterial, where there are a number of persons concerned, who gave the mortal blow; all that are present are in the eye of the law principals. This is a rule settled by the judges of England upon solid argument."

To the bar now stepped young Josiah Quincy to open for the defense. After a vigorous speech, in which he reminded the jurors that a soldier's life was, from a legal standpoint, "as estimable as the life of any other citizen," he began summoning witnesses to bolster his assertion that the soldiers had fired in self-defense. This was the climax of the Adams-Quincy tightrope act. Could the defense prove a mob was at work without pricking the jury's civic pride and political animosity? One by one the witnesses paraded to the stand.

James Crawford told how on the way home he met "numbers of people" going downtown with sticks in their hands. The sticks were "not common walking canes but pretty large cudgels." Archibald Wilson told of sitting in a house near Dock Square when "a certain gentleman" came in and asked how "he came to be sitting there when there was such trouble betwixt the soldiers and inhabitants." Looking out the window, Wilson saw thirty or forty men from the North End make "two or three sundry attacks up that lane where the barracks which are called Murray's were."

"How were they armed that came from the North End?" Josiah Quincy asked.

"They had sticks or staves, I know not what they are called," Wilson said.

In Dock Square Wilson found some two hundred men gathered. They surged away as if on a signal giving "two or three cheers for [*i.e.*, challenging] the main guard." Wilson followed them and was in Royal Exchange Lane, leading into King Street, when the bells rang. He said he heard voices shouting fire and remarked it was "uncommon to go to a fire with bludgeons." Somebody told him, "they were uncommon bells."

William Hunter, the next witness, added another

Dr. John Jeffries, star witness for the defense, later moved to England as a Loyalist. In 1785 he became famous when, with a French partner, he made the first balloon crossing of the English Channel.

significant detail to the gathering in Dock Square. He told of seeing "a gentleman" with a red cloak around whom the crowd gathered. "He stood in the middle of them and they were all very quiet; he spoke to them a little while, and then he went off and they took off their hats and gave three cheers for the main guard."

"Was the man who spoke to these people a tall or short man?" Josiah Quincy asked.

"Pretty tall."

"How was he dressed?"

"He had a white wig and red cloak, and instantly after his talking a few minutes to them they made huzzas for the main guard."

It may well have been at this point that John Adams arose in distress to interrupt his colleague and declare that he would walk out of the case if Quincy insisted on cross-examining witnesses to such unnecessary lengths, thereby setting the town in a bad light. (The transcript of the trial does not show us exactly where this happened but we know it occurred.) William Gordon, the British historian of the Revolution, describes the incident but mistakenly places it in Preston's trial. We must be grateful to him, nonetheless, because in John Adams' personal copy of Gordon's book he wrote an explanatory marginal note: "Adams' motive is not here perceived. His clients' lives were

hazarded by Quincy's too youthful ardor." Could anything sum up more graphically the terrible pressure under which Quincy and Adams worked? If Quincy persuaded a witness to identify the tall, red-cloaked speaker in Dock Square (Samuel Adams was short, but Will Molineux, his right-hand man, was tall), the Liberty boys in wrathful self-defense would have almost certainly unleashed the mob, jammed the courtroom, and created the kind of atmosphere that had convicted Richardson.

The evidence Adams did tolerate was bad enough, from the Liberty viewpoint. Witness after witness confirmed that there had been mobs of Bostonians surging through the streets, armed with clubs. Doctor Richard Hirons gave some details of a scene before the barracks. As early as seven o'clock some twenty or thirty townspeople appeared there, he said, led by "a little man" who lectured four or five officers of the 29th Regiment on the conduct of their soldiers in the streets. The man then began making a speech, shouting, "We did not send for you. We will not have you here. We will get rid of you." The officers insisted they were doing their best to keep the soldiers in their barracks and urged the speechmaker to use "his interest" to disperse the people.

Next came Benjamin Davis, Jr., who shattered the prosecution's claim that Samuel Gray was "in the King's peace" on the night he died. Young Davis told of meeting Gray, who asked where the fire was. "I said there was no fire, it was the soldiers fighting. He said, 'Damn it, I am glad of it. I will knock some of them on the head.' He ran off. I said to him, take heed you do not get killed . . . He said, 'Do not you fear, damn their bloods.' "

"Had he a stick in his hand?"

"He had one under his arm."

Now Quincy concentrated his fire on the scene in Dock Square. Patrick Keaton saw "a tall mulatto fellow, the same that was killed; he had two clubs in his hand and he said, 'Here take one of them.' I did so." Nathaniel Russell, chairmaker, said he saw trouble coming and "intended to retreat as fast as I could. I had not got three yards before the guns were fired."

"How many people do you imagine were then gathered around the party?"

"Fifty or sixty able-bodied men."

"Did they crowd near the soldiers?"

"So near, that I think you could not get your hat betwixt them and the bayonets."

"How many people do you think there might be in the whole?"

"About two hundred."

"Did the soldiers say anything to the people?"

"They never opened their lips; they stood in a trembling manner, as if they expected nothing but death."

This hit the prosecution so hard that they introduced a Crown witness, one John Cox, a bricklayer, who testified that he saw three soldiers threatening, earlier in the evening, to chop down or blow up Boston's sacred Liberty tree. They also threw in a future Revolutionary War general, Henry Knox, who said that Preston and his squad, while forcing their way through the crowd, behaved "in a very threatening" manner. "They said, 'Make way, damn you, make way,' and they pricked some of the people."

But the defense returned relentlessly to the evidence of riot. Benjamin Burdick admitted he stood in the front ranks of the crowd brandishing a highland broadsword. Newton Prince, a free Negro, told of watching people with sticks striking the guns of the soldiers at the right wing of the squad. Andrew, the Negro servant of Oliver Wendell, placed special emphasis on the conduct of Crispus Attucks. He told of seeing Attucks knock Killroy's gun away and strike him over the head. "The blow came either on the soldier's cheek or hat." Holding Killroy's bayonet with his left hand, Attucks tried to tear the gun loose, crying, "Kill the dogs. Knock them over." But Killroy wrenched his gun free, and Andrew, sensing imminent bloodshed, "turned to go off." He had gotten away "only about the length of a gun" when the first man fired.

"Did the soldiers of that party or any of them," Quincy asked, "step or move out of the rank in which they stood to push the people?"

"No," Andrew replied, "and if they had they might have killed me and many others with their bayonets."

Finally John Adams played his trump card, Doctor John Jeffries. Though he later became a Loyalist exile, Jeffries was one of Boston's most respected physicians. When Adams was representing America in London in the 1780's, he retained him as his family doctor. Jeffries told how he had been called to attend Patrick Carr, who had been mortally wounded in the firing. Carr lived nine days, and Jeffries conversed with him several times about the brawl. Carr told how he had been drawn from his boardinghouse by the ringing bells and had followed the crowd up Cornhill to King Street. Carr had not been in the front rank of the rioters. He was on the other side of the street circling the outer rim of the crowd when the guns began to fire, and obviously was hit by a wild bullet. Jeffries asked him whether he thought the soldiers would fire:

He told me that he thought that the soldiers would have fired long before. I then asked him if he thought the soldiers would have been hurt if they had not fired. He said he really thought they would, for he had heard many voices cry out "Kill them." I asked him then, meaning to close all, whether he thought they fired in self-defense or on purpose to destroy the people. He said he really thought they did fire to defend themselves; that he did not blame the man, whoever he was, who shot him. . . . He told me also that he was a native of Ireland, that he had frequently seen mobs and soldiers called upon to quell them: whenever he mentioned that he always called himself a fool, that he might have known better, that he had seen soldiers often fire on the people in Ireland, but had never seen them bear half so much before they fired in his life.

All by himself, Jeffries blew up ninety per cent of the prosecution's case. Proof of their consternation was the sudden production of additional witnesses at the very end of the trial. They were not particularly effective, merely reiterating what had been said before.

Josiah Quincy summed up for the defense. In a long, emotional speech he reviewed the evidence, urging the jurors to ask themselves crucial questions. "Was the sentinel insulted and attacked? Did he call for assistance, and did the party go to assist him? Was it lawful for them so to do? Were the soldiers when thus lawfully assembled, assaulted by a great number of people assembled? Was this last assembly lawful?" He closed with a moving appeal to mercy, quoting Shakespeare on the subject, asking the jurors to guarantee themselves "an absolving conscience" when the "agitations of the day" had subsided.

John Adams now took the floor to close for the defense. Thus far he had spoken little; Quincy had handled the interrogation of the witnesses. But everyone, jurors included, knew that Adams was the heart and head of the defense. His words would have a finality that Quincy, for all his emotion, could not convey.

Adams began with a direct and simple statement of his professional role: "I am for the prisoners at the bar." He would apologize for it, he said, only in the words of Cesare Beccaria, the eminent Italian jurist of the period: "If I can but be the instrument of preserving one life, his blessing and tears of transport shall be a sufficient consolation to me, for the contempt of all mankind."

In a quiet, matter-of-fact voice Adams proceeded to explain the law of homicide to the jury, and then applied the legal principle of self-defense to the situation of the soldiers in King Street, "with all the bells ringing to call the town together . . . [and] they knew by that time that there was no fire; the people shouting, huzzaing, and making the mob whistle . . . , which when a boy makes it in the street is no formidable thing, but when made by a multitude is a most hideous shriek, almost as terrible as an Indian yell; the people crying, 'Kill them! Kill them! Knock them over!' heaving snowballs, oyster shells, clubs, white birch sticks . . ." Consider, he asked the jury, whether any reasonable man in the soldiers' situation would not have concluded the mob was going to kill him.

Next he cited the law on riot: "Wheresoever more than three persons use force or violence, for the accomplishment of any design whatever, all concerned are rioters." Were there not more than three persons in Dock Square? Did they not agree to go to King Street and attack the main guard? Why hesitate then to call this so-called assembly a riot?

Perhaps at this point Adams saw the jurors' faces clouding. He swiftly led their emotions in the opposite direction by distinguishing between rioters and rebels. "I do not mean to apply the word rebel on this occasion: I have no reason to suppose that ever there was one in Boston, at least among the natives of the country; but rioters are in the same situation as far as my argument is concerned, and proper officers may suppress rioters and so may even private persons."

From 11 A.M. to 5 P.M. Adams examined the law and the evidence, frequently reading directly from authorities to bolster his arguments. The next morning he continued his summation, examining the testimony of various witnesses. He dismissed the Crown's attempt to prove Killroy's malice. "Admitting that this testimony is literally true and that he had all the malice they would wish to prove, yet if he was assaulted that night and his life in danger, he had a right to defend himself as well as another man."

The witnesses who had described Crispus Attucks' belligerent behavior were cited. Attucks was, said Adams, "a stout mulatto fellow whose very looks was enough to terrify any person . . . He had heartiness enough to fall in upon them [i.e., the soldiers] and with one hand took hold of the bayonet and with the other knocked the man down." It was to Attucks' "mad behavior, in all probability, the dreadful carnage of that night is chiefly to be ascribed."

Proving he could play on the prejudices of the jurors as skillfully as he could cite the law, Adams added: "And it is in this manner this town has been often treated; a Carr from Ireland and an Attucks from Framingham, happening to be here, shall sally out upon their thoughtless enterprises, at the head of such a rabble of negroes, etcetera, as they can collect together, and then there are not wanting persons to ascribe all their doings to the good people of the town."

The law, Adams declared, was clear. The soldiers had a right to kill in their own defense. If the attack on them was not so severe as to endanger their lives, yet if they were assaulted at all, the law reduces their offense to manslaughter.

Finally came a soaring peroration.

To your candor and justice I submit the prisoners and their cause. The law, in all vicissitudes of government, fluctuations of the passions, or flights of enthusiasm, will preserve a steady, undeviating course. It will not bend to the uncertain wishes, imaginations, and wanton tempers of men . . . On the one hand it is inexorable to the cries and lamentations of the prisoners; on the other it is deaf, deaf as an adder, to the clamors of the populace.

Once more Robert Treat Paine strove to rescue the prosecution's collapsing case. But he was in retreat all the way. "I am sensible, gentlemen," he began, "I have got the severe side of the question to conduct." He wasted time trying to justify the presence of so many armed citizens on the streets, renewing the argument that the soldiers had started the trouble first. He had nothing whatsoever to say about Doctor Jeffries' report of Carr's words, insisting instead on his witnesses' versions of the conduct of Attucks and Gray: "Attucks, fifteen feet off leaning on his stick, Gray, twelve feet off with his hand in his bosom." He ended by concentrating his fire on Killroy, calling his deliberate murder of Gray "beyond dispute." He all but gave up on the other soldiers in his closing lines. "You must unavoidably find him [i.e., Killroy] guilty of murder. What your judgement should think of the rest, though the evidence is undoubtedly the fullest against him, yet it is full enough against the rest."

The next morning, Justice Trowbridge charged the jury. It was a long and careful examination of the evidence and the law, most of which had already been covered by John Adams. But Adams must have stirred uneasily when he heard Trowbridge couple the words "riot and rebellion," and add a remark that the law in regard to treason should be "more generally known here than it seems to be." Judge Peter Oliver went even farther down this risky path. He declared that the riot had been perpetrated "by villains." As for the tall man in the red cloak and white wig, "that tall man is guilty in the sight of God of the murder of the five persons mentioned in the indictment."

Thus instructed, the jury withdrew. Two hours and a half dragged slowly by while the defense attorneys undoubtedly sat there fearing the worst. Finally, a door behind the bench opened, the twelve countrymen filed into their places, and the foreman, Joseph Mayo of Roxbury, arose to give the verdict. "William Wemms, James Hartegan, William McCauley, Hugh White, William Warren, and John Carroll: Not guilty. . . . Matthew Killroy and Hugh Montgomery, Not guilty of murder but guilty of manslaughter."

John Adams rose instantly and asked the benefit of clergy for Killroy and Montgomery. The judges dismissed the six acquitted men and quickly granted Adams' plea. ("Benefit of clergy," by 1770, had been interpreted to include anyone who was literate; and the "clergyman's" penalty for manslaughter was branding on the thumb.)

On December 14, Killroy and Montgomery were brought back to court. They read a passage from the Bible to establish their literacy, and prepared for the shock of the glowing iron. Adams recalled later he "never pitied any men more . . . They were noble, fine-looking men; protested they had done nothing contrary to their duty as soldiers; and, when the sheriff approached to perform his office, they burst into tears."

For Preston and the soldiers, the ordeal was over. They went their various ways, and John Adams saw only one of them again. Years later, when he was ambassador of an independent America to the Court of St. James's, he recognized Preston as he passed by on a London street. For bearing his part of the ordeal with patience and dignity, Preston, retiring from the army almost immediately, received a pension of two hundred pounds a year from the King. The enlisted men, as was their lot in those days, received nothing.

In his diary and later letters, John Adams maintained that his "disinterested action" in defending the soldiers was "one of the best pieces of service I ever rendered my country." Samuel Adams did not think so, at least in public. Writing under the name *Vindex,* he denounced the jury's verdict and the defense arguments in a series of scathing articles in the Boston *Gazette.* But Samuel Adams was a very subtle man. Privately, his friendship with John became even more intimate; early in the following year, when John Adams took his family home to Braintree and became a commuter to his city law office, he frequently ate breakfast, lunch, and dinner at his "brother" Samuel's house.

Did Samuel Adams realize that without John at the defense table, the trials might well have sent him and other leaders of the Liberty party, such as the man in the red cloak, to London under arrest for treason? Did the trials enable John to convince his cousin that the Liberty policy of violence had come close to destroying the cause, and must be modified henceforth? Both conclusions seem almost inescapable. But two years later, patient Cousin Samuel revealed another reason for his friendship. He had organized an annual extravaganza to commemorate the death of the Massacre victims with prayers and fierce anti-British oratory. In 1772, Samuel asked John to make the principal address. It would have been a most satisfactory way of including him at last on the Boston side of the case. But John Adams was still his own man. He quietly declined, explaining that he felt "I should only expose myself to the lash of ignorant and malicious tongues on both sides of the question."

There the matter would have undoubtedly remained if Parliament had not foolishly reignited the quarrel with the colonies the following year. The dead rioters thereby became enshrined in American folklore as martyrs. And John Adams was able to stand beside his Cousin Samuel with a clear conscience in the struggle against British oppression. That John won the larger place in history should not be surprising to anyone who penetrates beyond the patriotic myth to the interior drama of this great but little-understood trial.

For further reading: John Adams and the American Revolution, *by Catherine Drinker Bowen (Little, Brown, 1950);* The Legal Papers of John Adams, *edited by L. Kinvin Wroth and Hiller B. Zobel (Belknap Press, 1965).*

Statement of Ownership, Management and Circulation (Act of October 23, 1962; Section 4369, Title 39, United States Code)

1. Date of Filing: October 1, 1966
2. Title of Publication: AMERICAN HERITAGE
3. Frequency of Issue: Bi-Monthly
4. Location of known office of publication: 551 Fifth Ave., City, County, and State of New York, 10017.
5. Location of the headquarters or general business offices of the publishers: 551 Fifth Ave., N.Y., N.Y., 10017.
6. Names and addresses of publisher, editor, and managing editor: Publisher, James Parton, 551 Fifth Ave., N.Y., N.Y., 10017; Editor, Oliver O. Jensen, 551 Fifth Ave., N.Y., N.Y., 10017; Managing Editor, Robert L. Reynolds, 551 Fifth Ave., N.Y., N.Y., 10017.
7. Owner: American Heritage Publishing Co., Inc., 551 Fifth Ave., N.Y., N.Y., 10017. The names and addresses of stockholders owning or holding 1 percent or more of total amount of stock of American Heritage Publishing Co., Inc.: American Association for State and Local History, Nashville, Tenn.; The Society of American Historians, Inc., c/o Prof. Eric F. Goldman, Dept. of History, Princeton University, Princeton, N.J.; Charles Bruce Catton, Irwin Glusker, Oliver O. Jensen, Frank H. Johnson, Richard M. Ketchum, James Parton, individually and as Trustee under Declarations of Trust for James Parton III, for Dana Parton, for Nike Parton, and for Agnes L. Parton and a Child of the Grantor, Joseph J. Thorndike, individually and as Trustee under Declaration of Trust for Alan Thorndike, all of 551 Fifth Ave., N.Y., N.Y.; Virginia L. Thorndike, 520 E. 77th St., N.Y., N.Y.; Gerald P. Rosen, Game Cock Island, Byram, Conn.; Merrill, Lynch, Pierce, Fenner &

Smith, Inc.,* 70 Pine St., N.Y., N.Y.; Alexander Hehmeyer, 575 Madison Ave., N.Y., N.Y.; Arnold H. Maremont, 168 N. Michigan Ave., Chicago, Ill.; Roger S. Phillips, P.O. Box 11, Rowayton, Conn.; Shearson, Hammill & Co.,† 14 Wall St., N.Y., N.Y.; E. J. Stackpole, 220 Telegraph Bldg., Harrisburg, Pa.; Barbara Joan Straus, c/o Irving Trust Co., 1 Wall St., N.Y., N.Y.; John Thorndike, 11 Owenoke, Westport, Conn.; Evans & Co., Inc., 60 Wall St., N.Y., N.Y.
8. Known bondholders, mortgagees, and other security holders owning or holding 1 percent or more of total amount of bonds, mortgages, or other securities: None.
9. Paragraphs 7 and 8 include, in cases where the stockholder or security holder appears upon the books of the company as trustee or in any other fiduciary relation, the name of the person or corporation for whom such trustee is acting; also the statements in the two paragraphs show the affiant's full knowledge and belief as to the circumstances and conditions under which stockholders and security holders who do not appear upon the books of the company as trustees hold stock and securities in a capacity other than that of a bona fide owner. Names and addresses of individuals who are stockholders of a corporation which itself is a stockholder or holder of bonds, mortgages, or other securities of the publishing corporation have been included in paragraphs 7 and 8 when the interests of such

* Held for account of clients, no one of whom is believed to own or hold 1 percent or more of total amount of stock.
† Held for account of clients, one of whom, Dell Publishing Co., Inc., 750 Third Ave., N.Y., N.Y., is believed to own or hold 1 percent or more of total amount of stock.

individuals are equivalent to 1 percent or more of the total amount of the stock or securities of the publishing corporation.
10. This item must be completed for all publications except those which do not carry advertising other than the publisher's own and which are named in sections 132.231, 132.232, and 132.233, Postal Manual (Sections 4355a, 4355b, and 4356 of Title 39, United States Code).

	Average No. Copies Each Issue During Preceding 12 Months	*Single Issue Nearest to Filing Date*
A. Total No. Copies Printed (Net Press Run)	315,000	310,000
B. Paid Circulation		
1. Sales through dealers and carriers, street vendors and counter sales	1,000	800
2. Mail Subscriptions	299,000	300,500
C. Total Paid Circulation	300,000	301,300
D. Free Distribution (including samples) by Mail, Carrier or other means	3,700	2,000
E. Total Distribution (Sum of C and D)	303,700	303,300
F. Office Use, Left-over, Unaccounted, Spoiled after Printing	11,300	6,700
G. Total (Sum of E and F —should equal net press run shown in A)	315,000	310,000

I certify that the statements made by me above are correct and complete.
James Parton
Publisher

URILLA'S DREADFUL SECRET,

or
Four Out of Five Have It

A heart-rending excerpt from
Canto the Third of *Dentologia*,
a poem on the diseases of the Teeth

By SOLYMAN BROWN, M.A.

. . . Behold Urilla, nature's favored child;
Bright on her birth indulgent fortune smiled;
Her honored grandsire, when the field was won,
By warring freemen, led by Washington,
Nobly sustained, on many a glorious day,
The fiercest fervors of the battle-fray . . .

Her sire, whose freighted ships from every shore
Returned with wealth in unexhausted store,
Was doubly rich:—his gold was less refined
Than the bright treasures of his noble mind.

Urilla's sorry tale is part of a long, long poem published in 1833 by one of the founding fathers of American dentistry. It was brought to our attention by John W. Howard of the dental-school faculty at West Virginia University.

And she herself is fair in form and face;
Her glance is modesty, her motion grace,
Her smile, a moonbeam on the garden bower,
Her blush, a rainbow on the summer shower,
And she is gentler than the fearful fawn
That drinks the glittering dew-drops of the lawn.

When first I saw her eyes' celestial blue,
Her cheeks' vermilion, and the carmine hue
That melted on her lips:—her auburn hair
That floated playful on the yielding air;
And then that neck within those graceful curls,
Molten from Cleopatra's liquid pearls,
I whispered to my heart:—we'll fondly seek
The means, the hour, to hear the angel speak;
For sure such language from those lips must flow,
As none but pure and seraph natures know.

'Twas said—'twas done—the fit occasion came,
As if to quench betimes the kindling flame
Of love and admiration:—for she spoke,
And lo, the heavenly spell forever broke;
The fancied angel vanished into air,
And left unfortunate Urilla there:
For when her parted lips disclosed to view
Those ruined arches, veiled in ebon hue,
Where love had thought to feast the ravished sight
On orient gems reflecting snowy light,
Hope, disappointed, silently retired,
Disgust triumphant came, and love expired!

And yet, Urilla's single fault was small:
If by so harsh a name 'tis just to call
Her slight neglect:—but 'tis with beauty's chain,
As 'tis with nature's:—sunder it in twain
At any link, and you dissolve the whole,
As death disparts the body from the soul.

Let every fair one shun Urilla's fate,
And wake to action, ere it be too late;
Let each successive day unfailing bring
The brush, the dentifrice, and, from the spring,
The cleansing flood:—the labor will be small,
And blooming health will soon reward it all.
Or, if her past neglect preclude relief,
By gentle means like these; assuage her grief;
The dental art can remedy the ill,
Restore her hopes, and make her lovely still. . . .

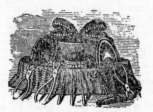